THE 22 IMMUTABLE LAWS OF BRANDING

Also by Al Ries and Laura Ries

The Fall of Advertising and the Rise of PR

Also by Al Ries

Focus: The Future of Your Company Depends on It

The 22 Immutable Laws of Marketing*

Horse Sense*

Bottom-Up Marketing*

Marketing Warfare*

Positioning: The Battle for Your Mind*

*With Jack Trout

THE 22 IMMUTABLE LAWS OF BRANDING

How to Build a Product or Service
into a World-Class Brand

**(This edition combines *The 22 Immutable Laws of Branding* and
The 11 Immutable Laws of Internet Branding
with added illustrations and text.)**

Al Ries and Laura Ries

Collins Business
An Imprint of HarperCollinsPublishers

This edition combines *The 22 Immutable Laws of Branding* and *The 11 Immutable Laws of Internet Branding* with added illustrations and text.

THE 22 IMMUTABLE LAWS OF BRANDING. Copyright © 2002 by Al Ries and Laura Ries. All rights reserved. Printed in the United States of America. No part of this book may be used or reproduced in any manner whatsoever without written permission except in the case of brief quotations embodied in critical articles and reviews. For information, address HarperCollins Publishers Inc., 10 East 53rd Street, New York, NY 10022.

HarperCollins books may be purchased for educational, business, or sales promotional use. For information please write: Special Markets Department, HarperCollins Publishers Inc., 10 East 53rd Street, New York, NY 10022.

FIRST COLLINS BUSINESS EDITION

Designed by Nancy Singer Olaguera

Library of Congress Cataloging-in-Publication Data has been applied for.

ISBN-10: 0-06-000773-7
ISBN-13: 978-0-06-000773-7

05 06 07 08 09 ❖/RRD 15 14 13 12 11

Dedicated to Mary Lou and Scott.

CONTENTS

INTRODUCTION

What is branding? From a business point of view, branding in the marketplace is very similar to branding on the ranch.

A branding program should be designed to differentiate your product from all the other cattle on the range. Even if all the other cattle on the range look pretty much alike.

Successful branding programs are based on the concept of singularity. The objective is to create in the mind of the prospect the perception that there is no other product on the market quite like your product.

Can a successful brand appeal to everybody? No. The same concept of singularity makes certain that no one brand can possibly have a universal appeal.

Yet, broadening the base, widening the appeal, and extending the line are all popular trends in marketing. The same forces that try to increase a company's market share are also the forces that undermine the power of the brand.

It's the difference between selling and branding. Could you sell a $100 Rolex watch? Sure, you could probably sell millions of them and in the process increase sales of Rolex watches. But what would happen in the long term to the Rolex brand? A cheap Rolex would ultimately kill the expensive Rolex brand.

The same principles apply to almost every aspect of marketing. In the short term, conventional marketing strategies (expansion and line extension) can increase sales, but in the long run they usually undermine the power of the brand and decrease sales.

Conventional marketing is based on selling when it should be based on branding. Marketing is not selling. Marketing is building a brand in the mind of the prospect. If you can build a powerful brand, you will have a powerful marketing program. If you can't, then all the advertising, fancy packaging, sales promotion, Web designs, and public relations in the world won't help you achieve your objective.

Marketing is brand building. The two concepts are so inextricably linked that it's impossible to separate them. Furthermore, since everything a company does can contribute to the brand-building process, marketing is not a function that can be considered in isolation.

Marketing is what a company is in business to do. Marketing is a company's ultimate objective. That's why everyone who works in a corporation should be concerned with marketing, and specifically, with the laws of branding.

If the entire company is the marketing department, then the entire company is the branding department.

As illogical as it might seem, we can visualize a time when the marketing concept itself will become obsolete, to be replaced by a new concept called "branding."

What is accelerating this trend is the decline of selling. Selling, as a profession and as a function, is slowly sinking like the *Titanic*. Today most products and services are bought, not sold. And branding greatly facilitates this process. Branding "pre-sells" the product or service to the user. Branding is simply a more efficient way to sell things.

That old expression "Nothing happens until somebody sells something" is being replaced by today's slogan, "Nothing happens until somebody brands something."

Take a supermarket or a drugstore with brands lined up on the shelves. A lot of buying takes place as customers pick and choose among various brands. But where's the selling?

The selling is in the brand. In this age of multimedia, the verbal endorsement of a product—essentially, its guarantee—is represented by the brand name rather than by the personal recommendation of a salesperson.

What has been true for years in the supermarket is now beginning to catch on across the marketing landscape. Except at the cosmetic counters, most department stores sell products without the help of a salesclerk. The sales-clerks are there to help ring up sales, period.

More and more car dealers are adopting the one-price, no-haggling Saturn strategy. Bookstores, pharmacies, bed-and-bath outlets are almost all self-service retailers. Even shoe stores are moving in that direction.

The retailing world is becoming one big Wal-Mart Super-center. Products are stocked in depth, artfully arranged, and reasonably priced, but never "sold."

There's a seismic shift taking place in the world of busi-ness. The shift from selling to buying. This shift is enhanced by, accelerated by, and caused by brands.

The essence of the marketing process is obviously build-ing a brand in the minds of consumers. But what, you may ask, is a brand?

Some managers believe that brands possess unique identities and qualities separate and distinct from their company or product names.

"They made their name into a brand," said one analyst about a company's successful marketing program.

They made their name into a brand? What does this state-ment mean? In truth, nothing. On paper, there is no difference between a company or product name and a brand name.

Obviously, marketing people have all sorts of definitions for company names, division names, brand names, and model names, not to mention subbrands, megabrands, flanker brands, and other variations.

When you look inside the mind of the prospect, however, all of these variations disappear. Imagine a customer saying to a friend, "What do you think of this new flanker brand?"

"Not much. I stick with megabrands or subbrands."

People don't talk that way. Nor do they think that way. To paraphrase Gertrude Stein, "A brand is a brand is a brand."

A brand name is nothing but a word in the mind, albeit a special kind of word. A brand name is a noun, a proper noun, which like all proper nouns is usually spelled with a capital letter.

Any and every proper noun is a brand, whether it's owned by an individual, a corporation, or a community. Patagonia is a brand name for a clothing line, but it's also a brand name for the tourist industries of Argentina and Chile interested in promoting travel to this pristine and beautiful place.

Philadelphia is a brand name for the leading cream cheese, but it's also a brand name for the City of Brotherly Love.

Brands are not limited to the 2.5 million trademarks registered with the U.S. government. Nor the additional millions of names and logotypes registered with other countries around the world.

Any proper noun is a brand. You are a brand. And if you want to be truly successful in life, you should consider yourself a brand and follow the laws of branding outlined in this book.

The power of a brand lies in its ability to influence purchasing behavior. But a brand name on a package is not the same thing as a brand name in a mind.

The customer who stops at a 7-Eleven to pick up a loaf of bread and a quart of milk usually ends up purchasing two branded products. Yet there might be little or no brand preference in the buyer's mind. It's just a quart of milk and a loaf of bread. Both commodity purchases.

Yet the same customer might also buy a six-pack of beer and a carton of cigarettes. Chances are high that the customer will search out a particular brand of beer and a particular brand of cigarettes to buy.

Conventional wisdom suggests that beer and cigarettes are different from bread and milk. Beer and cigarettes are brand buys. Bread and milk are commodity purchases.

While this may be literally true, it overlooks an important consideration. You can build a brand in any category, including bread and milk, as long as you follow the laws of branding. Some companies already have done so with brands like Lactaid in milk, Silk in soy milk, and Earth Grains in bread.

If there ever was a commodity category, it's H_2O, otherwise known as water. Since almost every person in America has access to good, clean water out of a tap, there is no need to buy water from a store, but many people do.

The brand name Evian is so powerful that the last time we bought 1.5 liters, we paid $1.69. That same day, on a per-liter basis, Evian was selling for 20 percent more than Budweiser and 40 percent more than Borden's milk. That's the power of branding.

What this book will help you do is to apply brand thinking or the branding process to your business. In other words, to turn your water into Evian, or yourself into the next Bill Gates. Aim high. You can never achieve more than you aspire to.

Since we wrote *The 22 Immutable Laws of Branding*, the Internet has arrived on the marketing scene. It's our opinion that the Internet will have an enormous impact on the way products and services are marketed. For example, 30 percent of all Southwest Airlines tickets are currently sold on the Web, 50 percent of all Dell computers are now sold on the Web, and an astounding 68 percent of Cisco's orders are currently taken on the Web.

The Internet is the ultimate in brand-centered buying. Consumers are purchasing automobiles from Websites without ever seeing the cars or going for a test drive.

What's happening in the automobile industry is also happening in many other fields. In financial services, for example, companies like Charles Schwab, E*Trade, Fidelity, and Vanguard are offering direct access, cheaper commissions, and on-line customer service, giving traditional stockbrokers a run for their money.

The Internet will have an enormous impact on the way products and services are branded. Why? One reason is that Internet brands are invisible. Before you can visit a Website, the name of that site first has to be registered in your mind. You can cruise the aisles of a supermarket and pick up brands that look interesting, but cruising on the Internet is a totally different story.

With millions of sites to choose from, you pretty much have to know where you're going before you embark on your Internet journey. You can, of course, start your journey at a search-engine site. But that's only a temporary solution. As more and more brands get embedded in the prospect's mind, why would anyone want to waste time checking in with a search engine when he or she can go directly to the site?

Why would anyone check out where to buy books at Yahoo! when you can go directly to Amazon.com? The Amazon brand was one of the first brands to be strongly registered in the mind of the book-buying public. But there are certain to be many more Amazon-like Internet brands to come.

How do you build a brand like Amazon.com? And furthermore, will brand building on the Internet be different from brand building in the real world? We think not. We think that all the laws of branding apply equally to the Internet as they do in the real world.

Recently, of course, the dotcom boom has become the dotcom bust. But is the Internet destined to go the way of the hula hoop? Hardly. In our opinion, most dotcom failures are branding failures.

- BarnesandNoble.com, Walmart.com, and Sears.com violated Internet Branding Law No. 1, the Law of Either/Or. None of these sites have done well.

- Pets.com, Garden.com, eToys.com, Furniture.com, Living.com, Hardware.com, Auctions.com, and hundreds of other sites violated Internet Branding Law No. 3, the Law of the Common Name.

- Free-PC, Freeinternet.com, and a host of sites based on giving products or services away in order to sell advertising have gone bankrupt. Why? They violated Internet Branding Law No. 6, the Law of Advertising.

And so it goes. You can't build a brand in the real world, and you certainly can't build a brand on the Internet, if you violate the laws of branding.

On the other hand, there are a number of big branding successes on the Internet:

- Amazon.com in books
- eBay.com in auctions
- Monster.com in jobs
- America Online in Internet service

What differentiates the winners from the losers? Good branding. And so we predict that those companies that follow the principles of Internet branding will be able to develop successful Internet brands . . . even though the Internet itself has become a graveyard of broken dreams.

Which is nothing new. In the past hundred years there have been some two thousand American automobile companies. Today, however, only two remain (General Motors and Ford). Does that mean that the automobile business is a bad business? Not necessarily.

In the past twenty-five years there have been some two hundred American manufacturers of personal computers. Today, two companies dominate the PC field, Dell Computer and Compaq. Does that mean the personal computer business is a bad business? Not necessarily.

So, too, with the Internet. Like any other high-profile industry, the Internet has attracted thousands (if not millions) of players. And most will fail.

If your company wants to be a powerful player on the Internet, then you need to study both the Internet itself and the laws of branding.

In addition, there are some unique circumstances about the Internet that pose special problems for branding. That's why we originally wrote the book *The 11 Immutable Laws of Internet Branding.*

Since the laws of branding apply equally to the real world and to the Internet, we feel that it would be helpful to have all the laws of branding in one convenient volume. Hence this book.

THE

22

IMMUTABLE
LAWS OF
BRANDING

1   THE LAW OF EXPANSION

The power of a brand is inversely proportional to its scope.

Think Chevrolet. What immediately comes to mind?

Having trouble? It's understandable.

Chevrolet is a large, small, cheap, expensive car . . . or truck.

When you put your brand name on everything, that name loses its power. Chevrolet used to be the best-selling automobile brand in America. No longer. Today Ford is the leader.

Think Ford. Same problem. Ford and Chevrolet, once very powerful brands, are burning out. Slowly heading for the scrap heap.

Ford buyers talk about their Tauruses. Or their Broncos. Or their Explorers. Or their Escorts.

Chevrolet buyers talk about their . . . Well, what do Chevy buyers talk about? Except for the Corvette, there are no strong brands in the rest of the Chevrolet car line. Hence, the brand-image problem.

Chevrolet has ten separate car models. Ford has eight. That's one reason Ford outsells Chevrolet. The power of a brand is inversely proportional to its scope.

Why does Chevrolet market all those models? Because it wants to sell more cars. And in the short term, it does. But in the long term, the model expansion undermines the brand name in the mind of the consumer.

MALIBU

WE'LL BE THERE

Chevrolet has been running separate advertising programs for each of its models, such as the Malibu, under the overall theme "We'll be there." Where do you buy a Malibu? You have to know that the mark is a Chevrolet trademark, and then you have to remember that the Malibu is made by Chevrolet. Most people won't bother.

1987:	1,500,398
1989:	1,348,430
1991:	1,161,236
1993:	1,049,618
1995:	1,054,071
1997:	980,554
1999:	884,749
2001:	830,038

Chevrolet car sales have fallen steadily as the brand lost its leadership to Ford. Today, Ford outsells Chevrolet by 18 percent. When you add in trucks, Ford's leadership increases to 23 percent.

In the credit card field, American Express is a distant third to Visa and MasterCard. Expansion is a dangerous strategy for any brand, but it is especially dangerous if you're an also-ran like American Express.

Short term versus long term. Do you broaden the line in order to increase sales in the short term? Or do you keep a narrow line in order to build the brand in the mind and increase sales in the future?

Do you build the brand today in order to move merchandise tomorrow? Or do you expand the brand today in order to move the goods today and see it decline tomorrow?

The emphasis in most companies is on the short term. Line extension, megabranding, variable pricing, and a host of other sophisticated marketing techniques are being used to milk brands rather than build them. While milking may bring in easy money in the short term, in the long term it wears down the brand until it no longer stands for anything.

What Chevrolet did with automobiles, American Express is doing with credit cards. AmEx used to be the premier, prestige credit card. Membership had its privileges. Then it started to broaden its product line with new cards and services, presumably to increase its market share. AmEx's goal was to become a financial supermarket.

In 1988, for example, American Express had a handful of cards and 27 percent of the market. Then it started to introduce a blizzard of new cards including: Senior, Student, Membership Miles, Optima, Optima Rewards Plus Gold, Delta SkyMiles Optima, Optima True Grace, Optima Golf, Purchasing, and Corporate Executive, to name a few. The goal, according to the CEO, was to issue twelve to fifteen new cards a year.

American Express market share today: 18 percent.

Levi Strauss has done the same with blue jeans. In order to appeal to a wider market, Levi introduced a plethora of different styles and cuts, including baggy, zippered, and wide-leg jeans. At one point, Levi's jeans were available in twenty-seven different cuts. And if you could not find a pair of jeans off the rack to fit, Levi's would even custom cut jeans to your exact measurements. Yet over the past seven years the company's share of the denim jeans market has fallen from 31 to 19 percent.

Procter & Gamble has done the same with toothpaste. When we worked for Crest, the marketing manager asked us, "Crest has thirty-eight SKUs. Do you think that's too many or too few?"

"How many teeth do you have in your mouth?" we asked. "Thirty-two."

"No toothpaste should have more stock-keeping units than teeth in one's mouth," we responded.

When we were asked that question, Crest had 36 percent of the market. Today the brand has more than fifty SKUs, but its market share has declined to 25 percent. And not surprisingly, Crest has lost its leadership to Colgate.

Many companies try to justify line extension by invoking the masterbrand, superbrand, or megabrand concept.

Colgate toothpaste is, of course, as line-extended as Crest. But what saves Colgate is its total focus on Colgate Total. This single-minded marketing program helped Colgate become the leading toothpaste brand in the U.S. market after trailing Crest for decades.

- Chevrolet is the megabrand and Camaro, Caprice, Cavalier, Corsica-Beretta, Corvette, Lumina, Malibu, Metro, Monte Carlo, and Prizm are the individual brands.

- Pontiac is the megabrand and Bonneville, Firebird, Grand Am, Grand Prix, and Sunfire are the individual brands.

- Buick is the megabrand and Century, LeSabre, Park Avenue, and Regal are the individual brands.

But people don't think this way. In their minds, most people try to assign one brand name to each product. And they are not consistent in how they assign such names. They tend to use the name that best captures the essence of the product. It could be the megabrand name. Or the model name. Or a nickname.

The Lumina owner will say, "I drive a Chevrolet." The Corvette owner will say, "I drive a Vette."

There are thousands of tiny teeter-totters in the consumer's

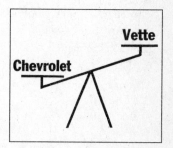

The owner of a Chevrolet Corvette will call his or her car a "Vette."

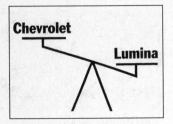

On the other hand, the owner of a Chevrolet Lumina will call his or her car a "Chevrolet." Double-branding a product is always dangerous. Whenever possible, a customer will simplify the brand name to a single word.

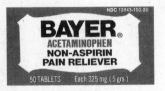

To compete with Tylenol, Bayer launched a similar acetaminophen product called Bayer Non-Aspirin. In the prospect's mind Bayer means "aspirin," so how could Bayer also mean "non-aspirin"? It couldn't, and the product went nowhere.

mind. And like their real-life counterparts, both sides can't be up at the same time. On the Chevrolet/Lumina teeter-totter, the Chevrolet side is up, so the car owner says, "I drive a Chevrolet." On the Chevrolet/Corvette teeter-totter, the Corvette side is up, so the Corvette owner says, "I drive a Vette."

Marketers constantly run branding programs that are in conflict with how people want to perceive their brands. Customers want brands that are narrow in scope and are distinguishable by a single word, the shorter the better.

But marketers, in an effort to distinguish their products from other similar products in the marketplace, launch ridiculously overzealous brand names:

- Vaseline Intensive Care suntan lotion

- Neutrogena oil-free acne wash

- Gillette ClearGel antiperspirant

- Johnson's Clean & Clear oil-free foaming facial cleanser

- St. Joseph aspirin-free tablets for adults

- Kleenex Super Dry baby diapers

- Fruit of the Loom laundry detergent

- Harley-Davidson wine coolers

- Heinz all-natural cleaning vinegar

Marketers often confuse the power of a brand with the sales generated by that brand. But sales are not just a function of a brand's power. Sales are also a function of the strength or weakness of a brand's competition.

If your competition is weak or nonexistent, you can often increase sales by weakening your brand. That is, by expanding it over more segments of the market. You can therefore draw the conclusion that line extension works.

But in so doing, the only thing you have demonstrated is the weakness of the competition. Coca-Cola had nothing to lose when it launched Diet Coke, because the competition (Pepsi-Cola) also had a line-extended product called Diet Pepsi.

While extending the line might bring added sales in the short term, it runs counter to the notion of branding. If you want to build a powerful brand in the minds of consumers, you need to contract your brand, not expand it.

In the long term, expanding your brand will diminish your power and weaken your image.

Unlike what many marketing people think, Tab was outselling Diet Pepsi by 32 percent the day that Diet Coke was introduced. (By keeping NutraSweet out of the Tab product and putting it in Diet Coke only, Coca-Cola effectively killed the Tab brand.) As a brand name, however, Tab is more powerful than either of the expanded names, Diet Pepsi or Diet Coke.

2 THE LAW OF CONTRACTION

A brand becomes stronger when
you narrow its focus.

Narrowing the focus is not
the same as carrying a
limited line. Starbucks
offers thirty different types
of coffee.

When you sell everything,
like a delicatessen, you limit
your ability to build a brand.
Name a national brand of
delicatessens? There aren't
any.

Every small town in America has a coffee shop. In larger cities and towns you can often find coffee shops on every other block.

So what can you find to eat in a coffee shop? Everything. Breakfast, lunch, dinner. Pancakes, muffins, hot dogs, hamburgers, sandwiches, pie, ice cream, and, of course, coffee.

What did Howard Schultz do? In an incredible burst of business creativity, he opened a coffee shop that specialized in, of all things, coffee. In other words, he narrowed the focus.

Today Schultz's brainchild, Starbucks, is a rapidly growing chain that does hundreds of millions of dollars' worth of business annually. His company, Starbucks Corp., is worth $8.7 billion on the stock market. And Howard Schultz owns a substantial share of that stock.

Every small town in America has a delicatessen. In larger cities and towns, you can often find delis in every neighborhood.

So what can you find to eat in a delicatessen? Everything. Soups, salads, hot and cold sandwiches, three types of roast beef, four types of ham, five types of cheese. Hard rolls, soft rolls, hero rolls, three types of pickles, four types of bread, five types of bagels. Potato chips, pretzels, corn chips.

Muffins, doughnuts, cookies, cakes, candy bars, ice cream, frozen yogurt. Beer, soda, water, coffee, tea, soft drinks of all varieties. Newspapers, cigarettes, lottery tickets. Every decent delicatessen prides itself on carrying everything.

What did Fred DeLuca do? He narrowed the focus to one type of sandwich, the submarine sandwich.

Good things happen when you contract your brand rather than expand it. The first stroke of genius in DeLuca's case was in coming up with the name.

Fred DeLuca called his chain Subway, a great name for a store that sold just submarine sandwiches. It was a name that no consumer could forget.

The second smart move concerned operations. When you make only submarine sandwiches, you get pretty good at making submarine sandwiches.

The average McDonald's has sixty or seventy individual items on the menu. Half the employees are teenagers, not yet old or mature enough to handle the complexities of today's operation. And people wonder why the food and service aren't as good as when McDonald's just served hamburgers, french fries, and soft drinks. (The original McDonald's menu had just eleven items, including all sizes and flavors.)

Subway has become the eighth-largest fast-food chain in the United States. The company has more than 15,000 units in seventy-five countries. Since Subway is a private company, we don't know exactly how profitable it is, but we do know how much money Fred DeLuca has been paying himself. (He was forced to disclose his salary in a court case.)

In 1990, Fred DeLuca paid himself $27 million. In 1991, $32 million. In 1992, $42 million. In 1993, $54 million. In 1994, $60 million. That's a lot of dough for making submarine sandwiches.

Charles Lazarus owned one store, called Children's Supermart, which sold two things: children's furniture and toys. But he wanted to grow.

What is the conventional way to grow? Adding more

Subway, with 12,008 units in the U.S. market, is second in size only to McDonald's, with 12,629 units. Like McDonald's, Subway has also taken its brand into the global market.

HAMBURGERS	15¢
CHEESEBURGERS	19¢
FRENCH FRIES	10¢
ROOT BEER	10¢
ORANGEADE	10¢
COCA-COLA	10¢
COFFEE	10¢
MILK	12¢
MILK SHAKES	20¢
CHOCOLATE, VANILLA STRAWBERRY	

Here is McDonald's original menu. You could buy everything on the menu, in all flavors, for just $1.56.

Toys "R" Us was the first specialty chain with a narrow focus. It served as a pattern for the "category killer" brands to follow.

After its initial success, Toys "R" Us went in exactly the wrong direction. It opened line-extension variations like Babies "R" Us and Kids "R" Us. Not only were these *spin-off* brands relatively unsuccessful, they also undermined the power of the Toys "R" Us brand.

things to sell. Sure, he could have added bicycles, baby food, diapers, and children's clothing to the store. But he didn't.

Instead, Charles Lazarus threw out the furniture and focused on toys.

Good things happen when you contract your brand rather than expand it. First he filled the empty half of the store with more toys, giving the buyer a greater selection and more reason to visit the store. Then, instead of calling it Children's Supermart, Lazarus called his place Toys "R" Us.

Today Toys "R" Us sells 20 percent of all the toys sold in the United States. And the chain has become the model for the specialty stores or category killers on the retail scene. Home Depot in home supplies. The Gap in everyday casual clothing. The Limited in clothes for working women. Victoria's Secret in ladies' lingerie. PetsMart in pet supplies. Blockbuster Video in video rentals. CompUSA in computers. Foot Locker in athletic shoes.

Good things happen when you contract rather than expand your business. Most retail category killers follow the same five-step pattern.

1. Narrow the focus. A powerful branding program always starts by contracting the category, not expanding it.

2. Stock in depth. A typical Toys "R" Us store carries 10,000 toys versus 3,000 toys for a large department store.

3. Buy cheap. Toys "R" Us makes its money buying toys, not selling toys.

4. Sell cheap. When you can buy cheap, you can sell cheap and still maintain good margins.

5. Dominate the category. The ultimate objective of any branding program is to dominate a category.

When you dominate a category, you become extremely powerful. Microsoft has 95 percent of the worldwide market for desktop computer operating systems. Intel has 80 percent of the worldwide market for microprocessors. Coca-Cola has 70 percent of the worldwide market for cola. And in order to dominate a category, you must narrow your brand's focus.

Why then do so few marketers want to contract their brands? Why do most marketers want to expand their brands? Because people look at successful companies and are led astray. They assume that companies are successful because they are expanding. (Starbucks, for example, currently is busy getting into everything from ice cream to bottled drinks to tea.)

But let's focus on you for a moment. Let's say that you want to be rich. Now ask yourself: Can I get rich by doing what rich people do?

Rich people buy expensive houses and eat in expensive restaurants. They drive Rolls-Royces and wear Rolex watches. They vacation on the Riviera.

Would buying an expensive house, a Rolls-Royce, and a Rolex make you rich? Just the opposite. It's likely to make you poor, even bankrupt.

Most people search for success in all the wrong places. They try to find out what rich and successful companies are currently doing and then try to copy them.

What do rich companies do? They buy Gulfstream jets. They run programs like empowerment, leadership training, open-book management, and total-quality management. And they line-extend their brands.

Will buying a Gulfstream V jet for $42 million make your company successful? Unlikely. Will extending your brand? Just as unlikely.

If you want to be rich, you have to do what rich people did before they were rich—you have to find out what they did to become rich. If you want to have a successful company, you have to do what successful companies did before they were successful.

> **Paper.**
> **Chemicals.**
> **Rubber products,**
> **including tires & boots.**
> **Electronics.**
> **Machinery.**
> **Computers.**
> **Mobile phones.**

Nokia once made everything. Then the company narrowed its focus to one product only, mobile phones. Today Nokia has 35 percent of the world's mobile-phone market and is the dominant brand.

Most companies can't leave well enough alone. Cafe Starbucks, featuring chicken potpie, was a Starbucks disaster.

Domino's not only focused on pizza, they also focused on home delivery only. As a result, Domino's became the second-largest pizza chain, only second to Pizza Hut.

As a latecomer to the pizza category, Papa John's found its narrow focus in an upgrading concept called "Better ingredients. Better pizza." Today Papa John's is the third-largest pizza chain in the United States.

As it happens, they all did the same thing. They narrowed their focus.

When Domino's Pizza first got started, it sold pizza and submarine sandwiches. When Little Caesars first got started, it sold pizza, fried shrimp, fish and chips, and roasted chicken. When Papa John's first got started, it sold pizza, cheesesteak sandwiches, submarine sandwiches, fried mushrooms, fried zucchini, salads, and onion rings.

Now how do you suppose Tom Monaghan, Michael and Marian Ilitch, and John Schnatter built Domino's Pizza, Little Caesars, and Papa John's into big powerful brands? By expanding their menus or contracting them?

Good things happen when you narrow the focus.

3   THE LAW OF PUBLICITY

The birth of a brand is achieved
with publicity, not advertising.

Most of America's 15,000 advertising agencies are committed to the concept of building a brand with advertising.

"The fundamental thing we're all about is building brand leaders," said the chief executive of D'Arcy Masius Benton & Bowles recently. "The way to do that is to have a superior understanding of the consumer, which leads to better, fresher, more powerful creative work that ultimately builds brands."

Building brand leaders with better, fresher creative work? We think not. Most marketers confuse brand building with brand maintenance. While a hefty advertising budget might be needed to maintain high-flying brands like McDonald's and Coca-Cola, advertising generally won't get a new brand off the ground.

Anita Roddick built The Body Shop into a major brand with no advertising at all. Instead she traveled the world on a relentless quest for publicity, pushing her ideas about the environment. It was the endless torrent of newspaper and magazine articles, plus radio and television interviews, that literally created The Body Shop brand.

Starbucks doesn't spend a hill of beans on advertising either. In its first ten years, the company spent less than $10 million on advertising, a trivial amount for a brand that delivers $2.6 billion in annual sales.

Anita Roddick created The Body Shop in 1976 around the concept of "natural" cosmetics, made of pure ingredients, not tested on animals, and kind to both the environment and the people indigenous to the communities in which the products originated. With no advertising, but with massive amounts of publicity, the Body Shop has become a global brand.

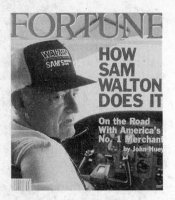

Brands don't create publicity. People do. Sam Walton, founder of Wal-Mart, was a master at getting media coverage. As a brand, Wal-Mart was built on publicity, not advertising.

There is absolutely no publicity potential in a brand of beer called just plain "Miller." In spite of a $50 million advertising investment in its first year, the brand died a quick death.

Wal-Mart became the world's largest retailer with annual sales of more than $200 billion with very little advertising. A Wal-Mart sibling, Sam's Club, averages $45 million per store with almost no advertising.

On the other hand, Miller Brewing spent $50 million to launch a brand called Miller Regular. (Or just plain Miller.) The brand generated no publicity, almost no perceptions in the minds of beer drinkers, and very little sales—$50 million down the drain.

Would better, fresher creative work have built a beer called Miller Regular into a brand leader? We think not. There is no publicity potential in a regular beer with a line-extended name like Miller.

In the past, it may have been true that a beefy advertising budget was the key ingredient in the brand-building process. But what worked in the past doesn't necessarily work today. We live in an overcommunicated society, where each of us gets hit with hundreds of commercial messages daily.

Today brands are born, not made. A new brand must be capable of generating favorable publicity in the media or it won't have a chance in the marketplace.

And just how do you generate publicity? The best way to generate publicity is by being first. In other words, by being the first brand in a new category.

- Band-Aid, the first adhesive bandage

- Charles Schwab, the first discount stockbrokerage firm

- CNN, the first cable news network

- Compaq, the first portable personal computer

- Domino's, the first home delivery pizza chain

- ESPN, the first cable sports network

- Gore-Tex, the first breathable waterproof cloth

- Heineken, the first imported beer

- Hertz, the first car-rental company

- Intel, the first microprocessor

- Jell-O, the first gelatin dessert

- Kentucky Fried Chicken, the first fast-food chicken chain

- *National Enquirer,* the first supermarket tabloid

- *Playboy,* the first men's magazine

- Q-Tips, the first cotton swab

- Reynolds Wrap, the first aluminum foil

- Rollerblade, the first in-line skate

- Samuel Adams, the first microbrewed beer

- Saran Wrap, the first plastic food wrap

- Sun Microsystems, the first Unix workstation

- *Time,* the first weekly news magazine

- Xerox, the first plain-paper copier

Silk was the first brand of fresh soy milk. Packaged like regular cow's milk and sold in the refrigerated sections of supermarkets, Silk has become a big success. Sales are approaching $100 million annually.

The New York Times is called a "newspaper," not a "betterpaper," because it prints what is new, not what is better.

All of these brands (and many, many more) were first in a new category and, in the process, generated enormous amounts of publicity.

There's a strong relationship between the two. The news media wants to talk about what's new, what's first, and what's hot, not what's better. When your brand can make news, it has a chance to generate publicity. And the best way to make news is to announce a new category, not a new product.

What others say about your brand is much more powerful than what you say about it yourself. That's why publicity in general is more effective than advertising. And why, over

1. Fleishman-Hillard
2. Weber Shandwick
3. Burson-Marsteller
4. Hill & Knowlton
5. Edelman
6. BSMG
7. Ketchum
8. Porter Novelli
9. Ogilvy Public Relations
10. Golin/Harris

One reason that publicity is often downplayed in favor of advertising is the fact that most large PR agencies are owned by advertising conglomerates. Of the ten largest U.S. PR firms, nine are owned by advertising companies. Only Edelman is an independent.

the past two decades, public relations has eclipsed advertising as the most effective force in branding.

Yet for years public relations has been treated as a secondary function to advertising. PR people even used to measure their successes in terms of advertising space. Publicity stories were converted into equivalent advertising expenditures.

Even worse, marketing strategies were usually formulated first into advertising slogans. Then the public relations people were asked to reinforce the advertising by creating PR programs to communicate those slogans.

Not anymore. Today brands are built with publicity and maintained with advertising. The cart is now driving the horse.

So why hasn't the ascendancy of PR made news in the media? Why are public relations departments in most companies still subservient to advertising departments? Why are nine of the top ten public relations firms still owned by advertising agencies instead of vice versa?

Why have the media ignored the biggest news story in marketing?

It's the grass phenomenon. Nobody ever notices the grass growing or pays attention to a trend that is slow in developing.

Take facsimile, for example. Over the past two decades, the facsimile has become an indispensable part of every company's communication portfolio. Americans will send 65 billion pages of faxes this year, more than 230 per person. And 50 percent of all international telephone calls are now fax calls.

Yet we don't remember a single article in any of the major management publications on the rise of facsimile. It happened too slowly.

On the other hand, the opposite is true of the Internet.

The rise of the Internet happened so quickly that it created a blaze of publicity, as did the rapid fall of Internet stocks.

Advertising executives in particular are inclined to slight public relations. "If the advertising is brilliant, the PR will fall out of that," said one particularly brilliant advertising executive recently.

But what works in branding today is publicity, not advertising. This is especially true in the high-tech field. All of the big global marketing powerhouses—Microsoft, Intel, Dell, Compaq, Gateway, Oracle, Cisco, SAP, and Sun Microsystems—were first created in the pages of *The Wall Street Journal, Business Week, Forbes,* and *Fortune.* By publicity, not by advertising.

Years ago we worked with Lotus Development Corp. on branding strategy for Lotus Notes. The essence of the strategy was the promotion of Notes as "the first successful *groupware* product." With, of course, the emphasis on "groupware."

This idea caught on like crazy with the media, which ran story after story on the new groupware concept. Yet typically the Lotus advertising people ignored the groupware idea in favor of nonsensical advertising pabulum.

It didn't matter because public relations is more important than advertising. As a result of the publicity program, Notes became an enormous success and ultimately IBM paid the astounding price of $3.5 billion for Lotus Development Corp.

Most companies develop their branding strategies as if advertising were their primary communications vehicle. They're wrong. Strategy should be developed first from a publicity point of view.

The Wall Street Journal has become a high-technology trade paper. If your company is not mentioned favorably and frequently in the *Journal,* you're not going to make it in the high-tech field.

A leader needs to promote the category, not the brand. As the leader in the new groupware category, Lotus Notes greatly benefited from articles such as this one, which appeared in *Fortune* magazine.

4   THE LAW OF ADVERTISING

Once born, a brand needs advertising
to stay healthy.

GOODYEAR

 # 1 in TIRES

A consistent theme of
Goodyear advertising over
the years has been "#1 in
tires." So who makes the
best tires? "It must be
Goodyear," thinks the
consumer. "It's the leader."

Your advertising budget is like a country's defense budget.
Those massive advertising dollars don't buy you anything;
they just keep you from losing market share to your competition.

All of its tanks, planes, and missiles just keep a country
from being overrun by one of its enemies.

Publicity is a powerful tool, but sooner or later a brand
outlives its publicity potential. The process normally goes
through two distinct phases.

Phase one involves the introduction of the new category—the plain-paper copier, for example, introduced by
Xerox in 1959. Hundreds of magazine and newspaper articles were written about the launch of the 914 copier. Xerox
executives also appeared on numerous television shows to
demonstrate their new baby. Much was written about the
potential of the new category.

Phase two concerns the rise of the company that pioneered the new category. Again, hundreds of articles were
written about the marketing and financial successes of
Xerox, a company that rose from the ashes of Haloid, a
manufacturer of photographic paper.

Today, everybody knows that Xerox pioneered xerography and has become a global leader in copiers. There's no news story left to tell, so advertising takes over.

Almost every successful brand goes through the same process. Brands like Compaq, Dell, SAP, Oracle, Cisco, Microsoft, Starbucks, and Wal-Mart were born in a blaze of publicity. As the publicity dies out, each of these brands has had to shift to massive advertising to defend its position. First publicity, then advertising is the general rule.

(Anybody who thinks advertising built Microsoft into a macrobrand should go back and read Chapter 3 again.)

Sooner or later a leader has to shift its branding strategy from publicity to advertising. By raising the price of admission, advertising makes it difficult for a competitor to carve out a substantial share of the market.

To attack a heavily defended neighboring country requires substantial military expenditures. To attack a heavily defended brand leader like Coca-Cola, Nike, or McDonald's requires substantial marketing expenditures.

Leaders should not look on their advertising budgets as investments that will pay dividends. Instead leaders should look on their advertising budgets as insurance that will protect them against losses caused by competitive attacks.

What should a brand leader advertise? Brand leadership, of course. Leadership is the single most important motivating factor in consumer behavior.

- Heinz, America's favorite ketchup

- Budweiser, king of beers

- Coca-Cola, the real thing

- Visa, it's everywhere you want to be

- Barilla, Italy's #1 pasta

- Goodyear, #1 in tires

So easy to use, no wonder it's #1

You can't go wrong, people think, by going with the leader. America Online reinforces its leadership position with the theme "So easy to use, no wonder it's #1."

Toshiba has maintained its leadership position in the portable computer field with advertising like this: "Take off with the best selling portables in the world."

The list of leaders that advertise their leadership is very short. Most leaders advertise some aspect of their quality.

But what happens when your advertising says, "Our product is better"? What does the reader, the viewer, or the listener to the advertisement really think when you make the claim that you produce a better product?

"That's what they all say."

Pick up a copy of any magazine or newspaper and flip through the advertisements. Almost every ad makes some type of better-product claim. That's what they all say.

But what happens when your advertising says, "Our product is the leader"? What does the prospect think?

"It must be better."

Who makes the best ketchup in America? Do you really believe Hunt's is the best? You might, but most people believe that Heinz is the best. Why?

Heinz is the leader and everybody knows that in this freedom-loving, democratic, equal-opportunity country of ours, the better product always wins.

"I pledge allegiance to the flag of the United States of America, the republic for which it stands, and the leading brand in each category."

As yet, we Americans don't do the pledge of brand allegiance, but we might as well. That's how strong our belief in the notion that the better brand will win.

Then why, you may ask, don't more advertisers advertise leadership? (Such claims are quite rare.)

They do consumer research. They ask customers why they buy the brands they buy. And people are quick to reply that they would never buy a brand just because it's the leader. As a matter of fact, they go out of their way to deny it.

"I never buy a brand just because it's the leader."

Then why did you choose the leading brand? Why do you drink Coca-Cola? Or rent from Hertz? Or drink Budweiser beer?

"Because it's better."

And now we have completed the circle. Everyone knows the better product will win in the marketplace. Since most people want to buy the better product, most people buy the leading brand. Which in turn keeps that brand the leader and gives that brand the perception that it's the better product.

Advertising is a powerful tool, not to build leadership of a fledgling brand, but to maintain that leadership once it is obtained. Companies that want to protect their well-established brands should not hesitate to use massive advertising programs to smother the competition.

Indeed, advertising is expensive. Today it takes $2 million or so to buy thirty seconds of advertising time during the Super Bowl. And top-rated prime-time shows are equally ridiculous from a monetary point of view. *ER*, for example, costs $620,000 for a thirty-second commercial. Then you have to add the cost of production, which has been averaging $343,000 per commercial.

So why spend the money?

Advertising may not pay for itself, but if you're the leader, advertising will make your competitor pay through the nose for the privilege of competing with you. Many won't be able to afford it; those who can won't bother. Instead they'll be content to nibble on the crumbs around your huge piece of the pie.

McDonald's	$627 million
Toyota	569 million
Visa	268 million
Budweiser	244 million
Nike	220 million
Coca-Cola	174 million
Tylenol	171 million

What do these brands get for their massive annual advertising expenditures? They don't get a good return on their investments. Rather, they get protection from their competition.

THE LAW OF THE WORD

A brand should strive to own a word
in the mind of the consumer.

What comes to mind when you think about owning a
Mercedes-Benz?

If you could pry open the mind of the typical automobile
buyer, you would probably find the word "prestige" closely
identified with the brand. Tell the truth, don't you associate
prestige with the Mercedes-Benz brand? Most people do.

You might also associate attributes like *expensive, German, well engineered*, and *reliable* with the brand, but the
core differentiation is prestige. Lamborghinis are expensive,
Audis are German, Hondas are well engineered, and Toyotas
are reliable, but none of these brands conveys the prestige of
a Mercedes.

If you want to build a brand, you must focus your
branding efforts on owning a word in the prospect's mind. A
word that nobody else owns.

What prestige is to Mercedes, safety is to Volvo.

Volvo owns the word "safety" in the mind of the automobile
buyer. And, as a result, over the past decade Volvo has become
the largest-selling European luxury car in America.

Once a brand owns a word, it's almost impossible for a
competitor to take that word away from the brand. Could
you build a safer car than a Volvo? Probably. Many brands
have already claimed to do so, including Saab, BMW, and

Volvo owns the word "safety"
in the mind of the car buyer.
Yet this position wasn't built
by advertisements like this
one. Rather, it was built by
publicity, especially Volvo's
invention of the three-point
seat belt and crushable body
construction.

Mercedes-Benz. Could one of these other brands own the word "safety" in the mind? Probably not.

What comes to mind when you think about owning a BMW?

A car that's fun to drive. The ultimate driving machine. BMW owns the word "driving" in the mind. And, as a result, BMW has become the second-largest-selling European luxury car in America.

Yet none of these three brands (Mercedes, Volvo, and BMW) is a perfect example of the law of the word since they have all recently violated the law. Mercedes has moved into less expensive, less prestigious cars. Volvo into sporty cars. And BMW into more luxurious cars.

And so it goes. The minute a brand begins to stand for something in the mind, the company that owns the brand looks for ways to broaden the base, to get into other markets, to capture other attributes. This is a serious error and one of the most common mistakes in branding.

What's a Kleenex? What word do you associate with the Kleenex brand?

On the surface, Kleenex seems unfocused. It's soft and pops up; it's well known and comes in many different forms. There are sport Kleenexes, family-size Kleenexes, psychedelic Kleenexes. Kleenex is by far the leading brand of pocket tissue.

What word does Kleenex own in the mind? Kleenex owns the category word. *Kleenex is tissue.*

Kleenex was the first pocket tissue. Before Kimberly-Clark introduced Kleenex, there was no market for a pocket tissue. But instead of expanding to toilet tissue and paper towels, Kleenex kept hammering away at its original focus.

"Don't put a cold in your pocket," was the marketing message for many years. The pocket handkerchief virtually disappeared from the market, replaced by Kleenex tissues in their many variations.

Why don't the many varieties of tissue dilute the Kleenex

The ultimate driving machine.

BMW owns the word "driving" in the mind of the automobile buyer. Unlike Volvo, advertising played a more significant role in the rise of BMW, although the brand greatly benefited from the publicity generated by its reputation as the favorite car of yuppies.

The ultimate word to own in the mind is the name of the category itself. When this happens, your brand becomes a generic brand. Kleenex is both the name of the brand and the name of the category. Lawyers hate generic brands, but marketing people love them. The truth is, many brands become generic in the mind, but few brands lose their trademark rights in the courtroom.

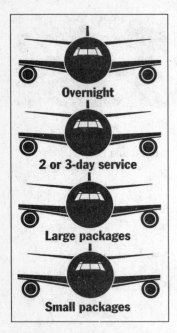

The air cargo leader, Emery Air Freight, offered all types of air cargo service. Whenever this happens, a leader becomes vulnerable to a more focused competitor.

Federal Express narrowed the focus to one service only, small packages overnight. As a result Federal Express became known as the "overnight" air cargo service and was ultimately able to own that word in the mind.

brand? Because when a person looks across a room, sees a box of Scott tissue, and says: "Please hand me a Kleenex," you know you have a solid brand locked into the mind of the consumer.

In the same way that Kleenex owns tissue, Jell-O owns gelatin dessert, Coca-Cola owns cola, Band-Aid owns adhesive bandage, Saran Wrap owns plastic food film, and Rollerblade owns in-line skates.

You know your brand owns the category name when people use your brand name generically.

"Make me a Xerox copy."

"I need a Q-Tip."

"Cover the plate with Reynolds Wrap."

"Hand me the Scotch tape."

Nor is it any secret how these brands managed to own the category word. They were first, plain and simple.

Here's the catch: You can't become generic by overtaking the leader. Pepsi won't become generic for cola even if the brand outsells Coke (as it once did in the supermarket distribution channel). You can only become generic by being the first brand and establishing the category.

So what do you do if you weren't the first in a category? Quite often you can create a new category by simply narrowing your focus.

Emery Air Freight, started in 1946, was the first air cargo carrier. But Emery fell into the Chevrolet trap. Instead of focusing on one type of service, it offered everything. Overnight, inexpensive two- or three-day service, small packages, large packages. "Whatever you want to ship, Emery can handle it."

What did Federal Express do? In the early seventies, it was a struggling player in the delivery business. But in a streak of brilliance, CEO Fred Smith decided to narrow its focus to overnight delivery only. "When it absolutely, positively has to be there overnight."

Today Federal Express is a much larger company than

Emery (now called Emery Worldwide). And "FedEx" has become the generic term for overnight delivery.

"FedEx this package to the Coast."

What word does Federal Express own in the mind? "Overnight," of course.

So what did Federal Express do next? It went global, where the very thing it had become known for, overnight delivery, is impossible. (Five o'clock in the afternoon in New York is already tomorrow morning in Singapore.) And it got into less expensive two-and three-day delivery. And it recently bought a trucking company.

Virtually every marketing move Federal Express has made in the last dozen years has moved the company further away from the overnight concept.

Does this expansion hurt the brand? Yes. Does it hurt the company? Maybe not, as long as there are no competitors astute enough to narrow the focus and put the same squeeze on Federal Express that Federal Express put on Emery Air Freight.

Look at what Prego did to Ragú. For years Ragú was the leading brand of spaghetti sauce with a market share in excess of 50 percent. Like Emery Air Freight, Ragú had many different varieties.

So what did Prego do? The brand narrowed its focus to one variety, "thick" spaghetti sauce. With this one type of sauce Prego won 27 percent of the market. Prego owns the word "thick" in the mind of the spaghetti sauce buyer.

The same principle holds true in many different categories, no matter how narrow or obscure the industry. In the financial world, a "Bloomberg" is a terminal that provides analytical tools as well as instant business news and stock prices. Bloomberg LP was the first company to introduce a device that would help money managers contrast and compare financial data.

Words are the key to brand building. Reality, of course, rests in a visual world of shapes, colors, textures, and

Ragú, the spaghetti sauce leader, expanded its line to six different varieties. As a result, Ragú became vulnerable to a more focused competitor.

Prego narrowed the focus to one type of spaghetti sauce, a "thick" variety. As a result, Prego was able to own the word "thick" in the mind and became a strong number-two brand.

**Full line
High quality
Great service
Low price**

You can't own everything. You might have a full line of high-quality products with great service and low prices, but how are you going to get all these ideas into the mind?

Federal Express became successful by expanding the market rather than by expanding the brand. Note the emphasis once placed on "overnight" in FedEx's packaging.

dimensions. But reality has no meaning without the context provided by the human mind. The mind gives meaning to visual reality by using words. Only when the mind thinks that an object is large or small, beautiful or ugly, dark or light, does that meaning arise.

The same is true of the product or service you are selling. The product itself might have a visual reality. But it's the brand name and its associations that give the product meaning in the consumer's mind.

So you can forget about the laundry list of wonderful attributes your product has. You can't possibly associate them all with your brand name in a human mind. To get into the consumer's mind you have to sacrifice. You have to reduce the essence of your brand to a single thought or attribute. An attribute that nobody else already owns in your category.

The average adult knows the meanings of perhaps 50,000 words. Yet there are about 2.5 million registered trademarks in the United States. And you want your trademark to stand for how many different attributes in the mind?

Until science figures out a way to replace human brain tissue with silicon chips, it's a physical impossibility for most brands to go beyond a single word. Consider yourself lucky if your brand can own a word like "safety" or "driving" or "thick" or "overnight."

Many marketers know this and they still look to expand the meanings of their brands. Why?

Growth. They feel trapped in their present positions. They want to grow, so they think they have no choice but to expand their brands.

But what works is not expanding the brand, but expanding the market. In other words, instead of moving from overnight to two- or three-day delivery, Federal Express expanded the market for overnight delivery.

By focusing on overnight, Federal Express was able to make overnight the in thing among business executives. As a result of its high price and flashy packaging, people thought, "Hey, this package must be important because it came via Federal Express."

And overnight deliveries boomed along with the fortunes of FedEx.

Mercedes employed a similar strategy. What was the market for expensive automobiles before Mercedes-Benz? Teeny-tiny.

Mercedes built the market for expensive cars by using prestige as its strategy. But you need subtlety in dealing with a word like "prestige." Its connotations may work in brand building, but the word itself does not. It's not that people aren't dying to own prestige brands. They just hate to admit it.

To be successful in branding a "prestige" product or service, you need to do two things:

1. You need to make your product or service more expensive than the competition.

2. You need to find a code word for prestige.

The first part was easy. Mercedes-Benz priced its vehicles at about twice the price of a comparable Cadillac. "Mercedes cars must be better than Cadillacs," thinks the buyer, "because they are twice as expensive."

Mercedes also found a powerful code word for prestige. "Engineered like no other car in the world."

What overnight did for Federal Express, engineering did for Mercedes. It expanded the market by giving the owner an excuse to buy an expensive, prestigious car. Instead of a Cadillac, the car of choice for the country-club crowd became a Mercedes.

But like Federal Express, Mercedes has also started expanding the brand with cheap sports cars, inexpensive sedans, and sport-utility vehicles. With a name like Mercedes-Benz, a reputation like Mercedes-Benz, and a history like

Mercedes: prestige

Mercedes-Benz owns the word "prestige" in the mind. But prestige is not a word that can be used in advertising, so the company had to find a code word for the concept.

Mercedes-Benz (the company invented the automobile), the brand should be the largest-selling luxury car in America. But it's not.

Go back in history. By far the most successful brands are those that kept a narrow focus and then expanded the category as opposed to those brands that tried to expand their names into other categories.

What was the market for expensive pens before Montblanc? Minuscule.

What was the market for expensive vodka before Stolichnaya and Absolut? Nil.

What was the market for safe cars before Volvo? Zip.

If "what is the size of the market?" is the first question your company asks itself, then you are taking the wrong road to success.

Ask not what percentage of an existing market your brand can achieve, ask how large a market your brand can create by narrowing its focus and owning a word in the mind.

6 THE LAW OF CREDENTIALS

The crucial ingredient in the success of any brand is its claim to authenticity.

Customers are suspicious. They tend to disbelieve most product claims. Your brand might last longer, require less maintenance, and be easier to use, but who will accept claims like these?

There is one claim, however, that should take precedence over every other claim. It's the one claim that elevates the brand above the competition. And makes every other claim much more believable.

It's the real thing. It's the claim to authenticity.

When Coca-Cola first made this claim customers instantly responded. "Yes," they agreed. "Coke is the real thing. Everything else is an imitation."

Even though the last "real thing" advertising ran almost thirty years ago, the concept has become closely associated with Coca-Cola. It's the brand's credentials.

Even today, "the real thing" is so closely associated with Coca-Cola that newspaper and magazine reporters will try to work these words into almost every article written about the company.

Credentials are the collateral you put up to guarantee the performance of your brand. When you have the right credentials, your prospect is likely to believe almost anything you say about your brand.

Many magazine and newspaper articles refer to Coca-Cola as "the real thing." The company makes a mistake when it doesn't use its "real thing" credentials in its advertising.

Leadership is the most direct way to establish the credentials of a brand. Coca-Cola, Hertz, Heinz, Visa, and Kodak all have credentials because they are widely perceived to be the leading brands in their categories. When you don't have the leading brand, your best strategy is to create a new category in which you can claim leadership.

Which is what Polaroid did when it became the leader in the new category of instant photography. Yet when it tried to tackle Kodak in conventional photographic film, Polaroid failed miserably.

Many marketers attribute Polaroid's failure to the fact that the brand couldn't be "stretched" from instant to conventional 35mm film. While true, this conclusion doesn't really describe the dynamics involved.

The simple fact is that Polaroid has no credentials in conventional 35mm film. Why buy your conventional film from Polaroid when Kodak is the expert in this category? Only if you want instant film will you buy Polaroid; it's the company that knows instant photography.

A number of years ago, Patrick Sullivan (currently CEO of SalesLogix) arrived in our offices with a software product called Act. "What does Act do?" we asked.

"Everything," Pat replied. "Act keeps track of your calendar, your correspondence, your mailing lists, and your expense accounts. Act literally does everything."

Not a good direction. We wanted to find the one thing we could use to build a new category. After much discussion the group decided that the new software could best be described as "contact" software. In other words, software designed for salespeople and others who do contact work.

"The largest-selling contact software" became the credentials for the new brand. Everywhere the brand name was used, the credentials were also used. In publicity, advertising, brochures, letterheads, calling cards. Even on the product box itself.

Act used its credentials, "the largest selling contact software," on everything, including the package itself.

Today, Act has 70 percent of the contact software market and has become the dominant brand in the category.

Credentials are particularly important in the publicity process. Reporters and editors are quick to dismiss advertising claims as puffery. But they readily acknowledge leadership and other aspects related to a brand's credentials.

- If a reporter is doing a car-rental story, who is he or she likely to call first? Hertz, exactly.

- If a reporter is doing a cola story, he or she will almost always call Coca-Cola.

- If a reporter is doing a computer software story, he or she will invariably call Microsoft.

Many companies run branding programs almost devoid of credentials. If you leaf through a stack of print ads or watch a series of television commercials, you'll find an endless parade of almost meaningless benefits: Tastes great, saves money, whitens teeth, easy assembly, bigger, smaller, lighter, faster, cheaper. While many of these benefits may be of general interest to prospective customers, they each lack credibility so they are generally ignored. "That's what they all say."

When the benefits, however, are structured around some aspect of a brand's credentials, they carry much more weight.

If Act claims to make you more productive on the road and cut your paperwork in half, then you tend to believe these claims because "Act is the largest-selling contact software."

Datastream did the same thing in maintenance software. Early on, Datastream found itself with 32 percent of the market. Granted the market was small. Very, very small.

No matter. Datastream promoted itself as "the leader in maintenance software." This same leadership theme was

Datastream	32%
CK Systems	4%
JB Systems	4%
PSDI	3%
DP Solutions	3%
HSB Reliability	3%
DFM Systems	2%
Comac	2%
Four Rivers	2%
Macola	2%

For many years Datastream not only called itself "the leader in maintenance software," but also gave market shares for itself and its competitors. With credentials like these, why would anyone want to buy maintenance software from any other company except Datastream?

used in all of Datastream's literature. Today, the market has exploded and Datastream still dominates the category. It truly is the leader in maintenance software.

Conventional thinking would have it otherwise. "The market is small. Nobody cares that we're the leader. They don't even care about maintenance software itself, otherwise they would be buying more of this kind of product. Forget leadership. We have to concentrate all of our efforts on selling the benefits of the category."

Never forget leadership. No matter how small the market, don't get duped into simply selling the benefits of the category early in the branding process.

There are also the long-term benefits of leadership. Because once you get on top, it's hard to lose your spot. A widely publicized study of twenty-five leading brands in twenty-five different product categories in the year 1923 showed that twenty of the same twenty-five brands are still the leaders in their categories today. In seventy-five years only five brands lost their leadership.

Never assume that people know which brand is the leader. This is especially true in fast-growing, new categories like contact software and maintenance software. Most new prospects have no experience with the category and little knowledge of available brands, so they naturally gravitate to the leading brand.

As the category matures, customers become more adventuresome and more willing to try different brands that offer seemingly unique advantages. Leaders often have to write off the more sophisticated customers who will go out of their way not to buy the leading brand.

Write them off. You can't appeal to everybody.

Not all brands can be leaders, although every category offers a wealth of possibilities. Take beer, for example. Here are some categories for beer leadership credentials:

- The leading beer

- The leading light beer

- The leading imported beer

- The leading microbrew

- The leading ice beer

- The leading high-priced beer

- The leading Mexican beer

- The leading German beer

- The leading Canadian beer

- The leading Japanese beer

For almost all of the hundreds of companies we have worked with around the world, we have found some credentials that could be exploited. If not, we created the credentials by inventing a new category.

You see credentials at work in everyday life. How many times have you walked away from a new restaurant because it was almost empty? Most people prefer to wait for a table at a restaurant that is crowded, rather than eat in an empty one. If this place was really good (goes the thinking), there would be a line out the door.

That's the power of credentials.

Asahi promotes itself as "Japan's No. 1 brand." This strategy is particularly effective in assuring distribution in bars, restaurants, and supermarkets. Why would any Japanese restaurant not carry "Japan's No. 1 brand"? What would that say about the restaurant itself: "We're not good enough to carry the leading brand"?

THE LAW OF QUALITY

Quality is important, but brands
are not built by quality alone.

What is quality?

Everybody thinks they can tell a high-quality product from a low-quality one, but in reality things are not always so obvious.

New Coke	55%
Original Coca-Cola	19%
No difference	29%

In blind taste tests, New Coke was strongly preferred to the original formula.

New Coke	13%
Original Coca-Cola	59%
No difference	28%

When consumers could see the brand names of what they were tasting, however, the original formula was strongly preferred to New Coke. Taste is in the brand name, not just in the bottle.

- Does a Rolex keep better time than a Timex? Are you sure?

- Does a Leica take better pictures than a Pentax? Are you sure?

- Does a Mercedes have fewer mechanical problems than a Cadillac? Are you sure?

- Does Hertz have better service than Alamo? Are you sure?

- Does a Montblanc pen write better than a Cross? Are you sure?

- Does Coca-Cola taste better than Pepsi-Cola? Most people seem to think so, because Coke outsells Pepsi. Yet in blind taste tests most people prefer the taste of Pepsi.

Common wisdom blames the testing procedures. If Coke outsells Pepsi, there must be something wrong with a taste test that shows the opposite.

Quality is a concept that has thousands of adherents. The way to build a better brand, goes the thinking, is by building a better-quality product.

What seems so intuitively true in theory is not always so in practice. Building your brand on quality is like building your house on sand. You can build quality into your product, but that has little to do with your success in the marketplace.

Years of observation have led us to this conclusion. There is almost no correlation between success in the marketplace and success in comparative testing of brands—whether it be taste tests, accuracy tests, reliability tests, durability tests, or any other independent, objective third-party testing of brands.

Read *Consumer Reports*. And then check the sales rankings of the brands tested compared to the magazine's quality rankings. You will find little correlation. As a matter of fact, the magazine's success could be attributed to its ability to find little-known brands that outperform leading brands.

In a recent ranking of sixteen brands of small cars, the number-one brand in quality was twelfth in sales. The number-two brand in quality was ninth in sales. The number-three brand in quality was dead last in sales. If quality translates into sales, the numbers don't seem to show it.

Let's say you went shopping for an automobile tomorrow. Does quality matter? Absolutely. Most car buyers look for the best-quality car they can afford.

But where does the concept of quality reside? In the showroom? No.

Quality, or rather the perception of quality, resides in the mind of the buyer. If you want to build a powerful brand, you have to build a powerful perception of quality in the mind.

As it happens, the best way to build a quality perception in the mind is by following the laws of branding.

Take the law of contraction. What happens when you narrow your focus? You become a specialist rather than a generalist. And a specialist is generally perceived to know more, in

New Coke was doomed to failure not because it didn't taste better than the original formula, but because it had the perception that it didn't taste better.

Quality is a constant theme of articles in the business press. Presumably, the way to build a quality brand is to build quality into the product. But success in the marketplace has little to do with the absolute quality of the brand.

As a company, GE is the most valuable company in the world. But as a brand, GE is relatively weak. In mainframe computers, for example, GE couldn't compete with the powerful IBM brand.

other words to have "higher quality," than a generalist.

Does a cardiologist know more about the heart than a general practitioner of medicine? Most people think so. Certainly the perception is true. From a marketing point of view, it really doesn't matter.

Yet most companies want to be general practitioners. Why? They want to expand the market for their products and services. And in doing so they violate the law of expansion.

Another important aspect of brand building is having a better name. All other factors being equal, the brand with the better name will come out on top.

Being a specialist and having a better name go hand in hand. Expanding a brand and being a generalist tend to destroy your ability to select a powerful name.

There is much misinformation on this subject in business publications today. Omnibus brands are weak, not strong. General Electric, General Motors, and General Dynamics might be well known, but as brands they are weak because they're too broad in scope.

We know what you are thinking. Some of these omnibus brands are among the world's leading companies in terms of sales, profits, and stock-market equity. And you're right. But a weak brand can in fact be a sales success if it competes with even weaker brands. Take General Electric. Most of GE's competitors are also omnibus brands like Westinghouse, General Motors, Siemens, and United Technologies. Who wins when two weak brands compete? A weak brand that just happens to be less weak than its competitor.

When General Electric tried to compete in mainframe computers with a strong brand like IBM, the GE brand was a multimillion-dollar loser. About $300 million to be exact.

When General Electric tried to compete in household appliances, the GE brand was no match for the specialists. (The products were subsequently sold to Black & Decker, which promptly proved that an omnibus brand like Black & Decker was no better than the GE brand.)

Mile-wide brands like General Electric and General Motors look strong, but in reality are weak. They look strong because they are well known and have been in business for decades. But when they go against the specialists, they are weak.

Another factor in building a high-quality perception is having a high price. Rolex, Häagen-Dazs, Mercedes-Benz, Rolls-Royce, Montblanc, Dom Pérignon, Chivas Regal, Absolut, Jack Daniel's, and Ritz-Carlton are all brands that benefit from their high price.

High price is a benefit to customers. It allows the affluent customer to obtain psychic satisfaction from the public purchase and consumption of a high-end brand.

The customer who wears a Rolex watch doesn't do so to be more punctual. The customer who wears a Rolex watch does so to let other people know that he or she can afford to buy a Rolex watch.

Why do blue jeans buyers pay $100 or more for a pair of Replay, Big Star, or Diesel jeans? And would they pay the same price if the label were on the inside of the jeans instead of on the outside?

And what does the sommelier say to the restaurant customer who has just ordered an eighty-dollar bottle of wine? "We have a twenty-dollar bottle that tastes just as good"?

Not likely. Even if the restaurant did have a twenty-dollar bottle that tasted just as good. And even if the customer believed the twenty-dollar bottle tasted just as good.

Conventional wisdom often advocates marketing a high-quality product at a comparable price. This is usually what is meant by a quality strategy. This is what Ford means when it says, "Quality is Job 1." Everything else, including price, is equal, but we are going to win by having the better-quality automobile.

Not likely. Quality is a nice thing to have, but brands are not built by quality alone.

A better strategy in a sea of similar products with similar

High price can be a benefit to customers. "The costliest perfume in the world" is the only message in this Joy advertisement.

Chivas Regal does two things to build a quality perception. Instead of eight years, it ages its Scotch whisky for twelve years. And it charges more money, then brags about it. "Go ahead. Spend the extra few dollars. It's Christmas, isn't it?"

Rolex has become the world's best-known and best-selling brand of expensive watch. Does quality have anything to do with its success? Probably not. Does Rolex make high-quality watches? Probably. Does it matter? Probably not.

prices is to deliberately start with a higher price. Then ask yourself, What can we put into our brand to justify the higher price?

• Rolex made its watches bigger and heavier with a unique-looking wristband.

• Callaway made its drivers oversized.

• Montblanc made its pens fatter.

• Häagen-Dazs added more butterfat.

• Chivas Regal let its Scotch whisky age longer.

There's nothing wrong with quality. We always advise our clients to build as much quality into their brands as they can afford. (Hey, it might save you money on service costs later on.) But don't count on quality alone to build your brand.

To build a quality brand you need to narrow the focus and combine that narrow focus with a better name and a higher price.

8   THE LAW OF THE CATEGORY

A leading brand should promote the category, not the brand.

According to the law of contraction a brand becomes stronger when you narrow its focus. What happens when you narrow the focus to such a degree that there is no longer any market for the brand?

This is potentially the best situation of all. What you have created is the opportunity to introduce a brand-new category.

- What was the market for an expensive vodka before Stolichnaya? Almost nothing.

- What was the market for expensive cars before Mercedes-Benz? Almost nothing.

- What was the market for cheap cars before Volkswagen? Almost nothing.

- What was the market for home pizza delivery before Domino's Pizza? Almost nothing.

- What was the market for in-line skates before Rollerblade? Almost nothing.

There's a paradox here. Branding is widely perceived as the process of capturing a bigger share of an existing mar-

EatZi's is the first brand in a new category which it calls "the meal-market." Jointly owned by Brinker International and Phil Romano, EatZi's focuses on restaurant-quality food primarily for takeout consumption.

Fresh Express was the "pioneer in packaged salads." The brand achieved a 40 percent market share by promoting the benefits of a new category.

You knew the Newton was going to be a disaster when Apple introduced the product with ads that said, "What is Newton?" If the manufacturer doesn't know what the category is, the prospect won't either.

ket. Which is what is usually meant when the newly appointed CEO says, "We have to grow the business."

Yet the most efficient, most productive, most useful aspect of branding has nothing to do with increasing a company's market share.

The most efficient, most productive, most useful aspect of branding is creating a new category. In other words, narrowing the focus to nothing and starting something totally new.

That's the way to become the first brand in a new category and ultimately the leading brand in a rapidly growing new segment of the market.

To build a brand in a nonexisting category, to build something out of nothing, you have to do two things at once:

- You have to launch the brand in such a way as to create the perception that that brand was the first, the leader, the pioneer, or the original. Invariably, you should use one of these words to describe your brand.
- You have to promote the new category.

"Isn't it easier to just promote the brand and forget about the category?" you might be thinking. Easier, yes, but not as effective.

When Apple introduced its ill-fated Newton, it forgot about the category name. At first it called the Newton a "PDA," for personal digital assistant.

A notebook computer, a digital cell phone, or a digital watch can all be considered personal digital assistants. PDA did not distinguish the Newton from all those other personal digital assistants on the market.

You knew the Newton was in trouble when Apple ran big advertisements with the headline, "What is Newton?"

Better to answer that question *before* you launch a new brand rather than *after*.

Customers don't really care about new brands, they care about new categories. They don't care about Domino's; they care about whether or not their pizza will arrive in thirty minutes. They don't care about Callaway; they care about whether or not an oversize driver will cut strokes off their golf scores. They don't care about Prince; they care about whether or not an oversize racquet will improve their tennis game.

By first preempting the category (as Prince did with the oversize tennis racquet, as Callaway did with the oversize driver, and as Domino's did with home delivery of pizza) and then aggressively promoting the category, you create both a powerful brand and a rapidly escalating market. Callaway Golf outsells the next three brands combined.

EatZi's is trying to do the same thing in the restaurant business. Average annual per-unit sales of the units in operation are an astounding $14 million. (The highest-grossing restaurant in the world is reportedly Tavern on the Green in New York City's Central Park, which does in the neighborhood of $35 million a year.)

With only a handful of units in operation, EatZi's has created an incredible amount of excitement in the restaurant industry. Yet the concept is simplicity itself.

Last year, Americans spent $207 billion on restaurant meals, a sizable market. Of that total, 51 percent was spent for takeout or home delivery.

What Little Caesars did in pizza, EatZi's is doing in high-end white-tablecloth restaurant meals: narrowing the focus to takeout only.

That's the way you build a brand. Narrow the focus to a slice of the market, whether it's pizza takeout or gourmet takeout. Then make your brand name stand for the category (the generic effect) at the same time that you expand the category by promoting the benefits of the category, not the brand.

What are the benefits of takeout pizza? It's the cheapest way to sell a pizza. No waiters or waitresses. No delivery trucks. As a result Little Caesars can sell a pizza cheaper than its competition. It captures this concept with its slo-

"Pizza! Pizza!" or two pizzas for the price of one was a brilliant strategy to promote takeout, a less-expensive way to sell pizza. Little Caesars was doing exceptionally well until they dropped this strategy.

By promoting the benefits of rotisserie chicken (better tasting, less fat), Boston Chicken initially was a big success.

Boston Chicken added turkey, meat loaf, and ham to the menu, changed its name to Boston Market, and went bankrupt. Subsequently the company was bought by McDonald's, which is trying to resurrect the brand.

EatZi's needs to verbalize the benefits of restaurant-quality takeout food. Our suggestion: "The joy of not cooking."

gan, "Pizza! Pizza!" Or the promise of two pizzas for the price of one.

EatZi's has yet to conceptualize the benefits of takeout beef Wellington, but that's what it should be working on. Promote the category, not the brand. What EatZi's calls the "meal-market" category.

When you're first, you can preempt the category. You are the only brand associated with the concept. You have a powerful publicity platform. You need to put your branding dollars behind the concept itself, so the concept will take off, pulling the brand along with it.

What happens when competition appears, as it inevitably does? Most category leaders just can't wait to shift into a brand-building mode. That's a mistake. Leaders should continue to promote the category, to increase the size of the pie rather than their slice of the pie.

Boston Chicken was a huge hit when it opened its doors. It was the first fast-food restaurant to focus on rotisserie chicken for the take-home dinner market. But instead of continuing to promote rotisserie chicken, it changed its name to Boston Market, added turkey, meatloaf, and ham to the menu, and fell into trouble.

Leaders get antsy as their 100 percent share of the initial market drops to 90 and then to 80 or 70 percent as the market grows. "We've got to fight back and recapture our rightful share," they say.

The rightful share of a leading brand is never more than 50 percent. There's always room for a second brand and a passel of lesser brands. Instead of fighting competitive brands, a leader should fight competitive categories.

"Take the bus," category leader Greyhound once said, "and leave the driving to us."

"Take home your meals from EatZi's," the meal-market category leader could say, "and leave the cooking to us."

Contrary to popular belief, what would help EatZi's (and

every category pioneer) is competition. Even though the leader's market share might decline, the rise of competitive brands can stimulate consumer interest in the category.

One of Polaroid's biggest mistakes was forcing Kodak out of the instant-photography market. Although it won a few million in its lawsuit, Polaroid effectively removed a competitor that could have greatly expanded the market. (A Coke/Pepsi advertising war benefits both brands. It attracts media attention, which expands the consumer's interest in the cola category.)

Years ago, Johnson & Johnson, the leading brand of baby shampoo, mounted a major marketing campaign to sell the merits of its shampoo to adults. "You wash your hair every day, you need a mild shampoo. And what shampoo could be milder than a baby shampoo?"

Brilliant. At one point Johnson & Johnson baby shampoo became the number-one brand of adult shampoo. If other baby shampoo brands had jumped on the adult bandwagon, sales might have gone even higher.

Unfortunately for Johnson & Johnson, there *were* no other major baby shampoo brands.

Leading brands should promote the category, not the brand.

THE LAW OF THE NAME

In the long run a brand is nothing
more than a name.

XEROX

One of the world's best-
known brands, Xerox
demonstrates many of the
most important laws of
branding, including being
the first in a new category
(plain-paper copier) with a
short, unique name. Yet
when Xerox tried to put its
powerful copier name on
computers, the result was
billions in losses.

The most important branding decision you will ever make is
what to name your product or service. Because in the long
run a brand is nothing more than a name.

Don't confuse what makes a brand successful in the
short term with what makes a brand successful in the long
term.

In the short term, a brand needs a unique idea or concept to survive. It needs to be first in a new category. It
needs to own a word in the mind.

But in the long term, the unique idea or concept disap-
pears. All that is left is the difference between your brand
name and the brand names of your competitors.

Xerox was the first plain-paper copier. This unique idea
built the powerful Xerox brand in the mind. But today all
copiers are plain-paper copiers. The difference between
brands is not in the products, but in the product names. Or
rather the perception of the names.

In the beginning it was easy to sell a Xerox 914 copier.
All you had to do was show the difference between a Xerox
copy and an ordinary copy. The Xerox copy was cleaner,
sharper, and easier to read. The paper lay flat, felt better,
and was much easier to handle and sort.

Today those differences are gone, but Xerox is still the best brand by far in the copier field. One reason is the name itself.

It's short, unique, and connotes high technology. The most valuable asset of the Xerox Corporation is the Xerox name itself.

Yet marketers often disparage the importance of the name. "What really counts is the product itself and the benefits the product provides to our customers and prospects."

So they come up with generic names like Paper Master. "What does a name like Xerox mean anyhow? Nothing. A name like Paper Master, on the other hand, helps us communicate the benefits of a better copier."

Even worse, they introduce the new brand as a line extension. "Nobody has ever heard of Xerox, a name that somebody just invented. On the other hand our firm, the Haloid Company, was founded in 1906. We have thousands of customers and a good reputation. Let's call our new plain-paper copier the Haloid Paper Master."

"Well," you might be thinking, "I would never make a mistake like that. I would never call a new product with as much potential as the 914 copier the 'Haloid Paper Master.' "

In retrospect, no. In futurespect, maybe you would. At least the vast majority of the companies we have worked with almost always prefer line-extended generic names to unique new brand names.

On a global scale, this is the biggest issue in the business community. Companies are divided into two camps: those who believe that the essence of business success is in the continuing development of superior products and services, and those who believe in branding. The product versus the brand.

The product camp dominates the marketing scene. "The brand name doesn't matter. What counts is how the product performs."

As proof of this principle, product campers are quick to

reduce the argument to absurdity. "If the product is no good, the product will fail regardless of whether the product has a good brand name or not."

Is a Xerox copier better than a Canon copier? How does a Ricoh copier compare with a Sharp copier?

Have you ever bought a copier? Which brand of copier is no good? Forget copiers. Which brands of any products are no good?

Sure, some people will dump on some brands. They might even say things like "I'd never buy a Jaguar." But these opinions are seldom universal.

The no-good product is the red herring of marketing. It is constantly being used to justify the no-brand strategies of most companies.

We don't mean literally a no-brand strategy. A company might own brands that might be called brands from a legal point of view in the sense that their names are registered trademarks. But the company's strategies are based on building the better product or service, and the brand names it uses to accompany these products have little power in the prospect's mind.

Product campers dominate the East Asia economy. Virtually every Asian company uses a megabrand, masterbrand, or line-extension strategy.

What's a Mitsubishi? Sixteen of the one hundred largest Japanese companies market products and services under the Mitsubishi name. Everything from automobiles to semiconductors to consumer electronics. From space equipment to transport systems.

What's a Matsushita? Same problem as Mitsubishi. Eight of the one hundred largest Japanese companies market products and services under the Matsushita name. Everything from electric equipment to electronic products and components. From batteries to refrigeration equipment.

Mitsubishi Corporation
Mitsubishi Electric
Mitsubishi Motors
Mitsubishi Heavy Indus.
Mitsubishi Chemical
Mitsubishi Oil
Mitsubishi Materials
Mitsubishi Estate
Mitsubishi Rayon
Mitsubishi Gas Chemical
Mitsubishi Paper
Mitsubishi Electric Bldg.
Mitsubishi Plastics
Mitsubishi Logistics
Mitsubishi Paper Sales
Mitsubishi Construction

Sixteen out of the one hundred largest companies in Japan use the Mitsubishi name. How can you build a Mitsubishi brand if its name means everything?

What's a Mitsui? Same problem as Matsushita. Eight of the one hundred largest Japanese companies market products and services under the Mitsui name.

Compare Japan with the United States. In a recent year, the top hundred companies in the United States had sales of $3.2 trillion. In the same year, the top hundred companies in Japan had sales of $2.6 trillion. Not that much difference.

The real difference is in profits. The one hundred American companies had profits on average of 6.2 percent of sales. The one hundred Japanese companies had profits on average of just 0.8 percent of sales.

That 0.8 percent is the average net profit in Japan. With so many companies close to the break-even point, you can be sure that many are losing money on a regular basis.

The Asian practice of fielding a wide variety of products under the same brand name has drawn favorable comments from many business writers who don't always look under the financial covers to find the real story.

Korea is in even worse shape. In a recent year, the sixty-three largest Korean companies had sales of $409 billion, but had a combined net loss of 0.4 percent of sales.

Take Hyundai, for example. This $71 billion Korean *chaebol* brags about a "chips to ships" strategy. Hyundai makes microprocessors, telecommunications satellites, passenger cars, commercial vehicles, subways, high-speed trains, turnkey engineering and construction projects, super-tankers, and LNG carriers, among other products. All under the Hyundai name.

Hyundai makes everything except money.

Throughout Asia you see the same pattern. Rampant line extensions that are destroying brands. (When you expand a brand, you reduce its power. When you contract a brand, you increase its power.)

Brands are not just something to think about at market-

Samsung
Hyundai
Daewoo
LG
Ssangyong
Hanwha

From a name point of view, Korea is in even worse shape than Japan. These six *chaebols* account for the bulk of the country's output.

ing meetings. Brands are the essence of the company itself. A company's very existence depends on building brands in the mind. And so does a country's.

East Asia does not have a banking problem, a financial problem, a monetary problem, or a political problem.

East Asia has a branding problem.

10 THE LAW OF EXTENSIONS

The easiest way to destroy a brand is
to put its name on everything.

You don't have to go to Asia to find examples of rampant
line extension.

More than 90 percent of all new products introduced in
the U.S. grocery and drug trade are line extensions. Which
is the major reason that stores are choked with brands.
(There are 1,300 shampoos, 200 cereals, 250 soft drinks.)

Scanner data indicates that many of those line extensions (at least in supermarkets) sit on the shelf and gather
dust. Research from Kroger supermarkets in Columbus,
Ohio, found that of the average 23,000 items in a store,
6,700 sold in a day, 13,600 sold in a week, and 17,500 sold in
a month, leaving 5,500 that sold nothing in an entire month.

This plethora of line extensions, in our opinion, is the
reason for the increased demands from retailers for trade
promotions, slotting fees, and return privileges.

According to industry experts, power has been shifting
from manufacturers to retailers. The primary reason is line
extension. With so many products to choose from, retailers
can force manufacturers to pay for the privilege of getting
their products on the shelf. If one company won't pay, the
retailer can always find another company that will.

No industry is as line-extended as the beer industry.
Before the launch of Miller Lite in the mid-seventies, there

In the mid-1970s
Budweiser, Coors, and
Miller dominated the beer
business. Thanks to line
extensions, these three
brands have become
fourteen today. Has per-
capita beer consumption
increased in the past
twenty-five years? No, it
has remained flat. The only
increase that has taken
place is in beer brands.

were three major beer brands: Budweiser, Miller High Life, and Coors Banquet.

Today these three brands have become fourteen: Budweiser, Bud Light, Bud Dry, Bud Ice, Miller High Life, Miller Lite, Miller Genuine Draft, Miller Genuine Draft Light, Miller Reserve, Miller Reserve Light, Miller Reserve Amber Ale, Coors, Coors Light, and Coors Extra Gold.

Have these fourteen brands increased their market share over that obtained by the original three brands? Not really. There has been some increase, but no greater than what you might expect. Big brands always put pressure on smaller brands, in the same way that Coke and Pepsi have eroded the market share of Royal Crown Cola.

Has the availability of these fourteen varieties of Budweiser, Miller, and Coors increased beer consumption? No. Per capita beer consumption over the past twenty-five years has been relatively flat. (Cola consumption in the same period of time has almost doubled.)

When your customers are not exactly rushing out to buy your product, why would you need more brands to satisfy those customers? Logic suggests you would need fewer brands.

But that's customer logic. Manufacturer logic is different. If volume is going nowhere, the manufacturer concludes it needs more brands to maintain or increase sales. When a category is increasing in sales, there are opportunities for new brands, but manufacturer logic suggests they're not needed. "We are doing great, we don't need any more brands."

As a result, the marketplace is filled with line extensions in areas where they are not needed and is starved for new brands in areas where they *are* needed. Figure that one out.

Another reason for the rise in line extensions is a company's natural instinct to copy the competition. Miller's introduction of Miller Lite was quickly followed by Schlitz Light, Coors Light, Bud Light, Busch Light, Michelob Light, and Pabst Light. The light list is endless.

One of the loonier line extensions of recent years was the 1993 launch of Miller Clear. The brand lasted for less than six months.

It's painful to remember and so hard to forget. After the introduction of Miller Lite, we rushed around the brewing industry with a simple message: Keep your beer brand focused on the regular market. That will give you a leg up on Joe Sixpack, who consumes an awful lot of beer. (You can see how successful we were with our message.)

Why did Miller introduce Miller Regular, a brand which most beer drinkers have never heard of? Because Anheuser-Busch has regular Budweiser, Coors has regular Coors, and Miller didn't have a regular beer.

Don't laugh. This is the way companies think. The competition must know something we don't know. Let's do the same thing.

One reason 90 percent of all new brands are line extensions is that management measures results with the wrong end of the ruler. It measures only the success of the extension. It never measures the erosion of the core brand.

And it's not just the erosion, it's also the lost opportunities. Big powerful brands should have market shares approaching 50 percent, like Coca-Cola, Heinz, Pop-Tarts, Jell-O, and Gerber's. But it's hard to find more than a few such brands. Most big brands have been line-extended to death.

- Budweiser (all varieties combined) has about 30 percent of the beer market.

- Marlboro (a brand that comes in at least a dozen different varieties, including Marlboro Lights, Marlboro Medium, and Marlboro Menthol) has only 30 percent of the cigarette market.

- IBM has only 6 percent of the personal computer market.

When Coors was planning the introduction of Coors Light, we asked one of its executives, "Where is the Coors Light business going to come from?"

More is not necessarily more. Marlboro is available in more than a dozen varieties, yet the brand has only 30 percent of the cigarette market.

In the past decade, Budweiser sales have declined almost every year while Bud Light sales have increased. (Bud Light is on the verge of overtaking Budweiser.) It doesn't take a marketing genius to know that Budweiser drinkers have been shifting to Bud Light.

Coors water? Do you suppose they wash out the beer barrels and then bottle the wash water?

Diet Coke may turn out to be one of the most monumental marketing mistakes ever made. The Coca-Cola Company didn't need a new diet cola—they already had the leading diet cola brand, Tab. Diet Coke is flat or declining in sales. (Mountain Dew has passed it to become the third-largest-selling soft drink after Coca-Cola Classic and Pepsi-Cola.) How long can a sugared product like Coca-Cola continue to dominate the soft-drink market? A transition from Coca-Cola to Tab would have been much easier than one from Coke to Diet Coke because Tab doesn't carry the negative baggage of a diet name.

"Oh, we're going to take it away from Budweiser and Miller."

When Budweiser was planning the introduction of Bud Light, the targets were Miller and Coors.

When Miller was planning the introduction of Miller Lite, the targets were Budweiser and Coors.

Maybe this concept is too complicated for the average CEO to understand, but isn't the Coors Light drinker more likely to come from Coors? And the Bud Light drinker from Budweiser? And the Miller Lite drinker from Miller High Life?

Certainly the numbers substantiate this conclusion. Since the introduction of the three lights, the three regular beer brands have all declined substantially.

(And what can you say about Coors Rocky Mountain Spring Water? Born in 1990. Died in 1992. Mourned by no one. Not too many beer drinkers wanted to shift from beer to water.)

The market, you might be thinking, is shifting from regular to light beer. That's true. But it's really two markets, and the best way to capture those two markets is with two brands.

But there are no major beer brands that are not line-extended, you might have concluded. And you're right. And what a wonderful opportunity for someone who understands the laws of branding.

Actually, until a short time ago, there was one: Amstel Light, which became the leading brand of imported light beer. So what did Heineken USA, the importer of Amstel Light, do next? It introduced Amstel Bier (regular beer) and Amstel 1870 beer.

Who drinks Diet Coke and Diet Pepsi? Do you really suppose that these diet cola drinkers used to drink beer, ginger ale, or orange juice? We don't.

Diet Coke comes out of Coca-Cola's hide. Sure, the diet

cola market has boomed, thanks to the public's interest in low-calorie products. But what Coca-Cola should have done was launch a second brand.

Actually it did. After the success of Diet Pepsi, Coca-Cola launched Tab. And Tab was doing quite well. The day Diet Coke was introduced, Tab was leading Diet Pepsi in market share by about 32 percent.

Now which is the better name: Diet Pepsi or Tab? If line extension is the superior way to build a brand, why did Tab lead Diet Pepsi by nearly a third?

Of course, Coke nearly killed Tab by keeping Nutrasweet out of the brand and only using it in Diet Coke. But you can't squeeze a good idea out of the marketplace. Tab still hangs in there with almost no promotional support.

When the low-fat craze hit the cookie market, almost every brand rushed out with a line-extended version of its regular cookie. As a matter of fact, the first fat-free cookie and early leader was Nabisco's Fat Free Fig Newtons.

Nabisco also launched a new brand of fat-free cookie called SnackWell's. Fat Free Fig Newtons were only a modest success, while SnackWell's became the seventh-largest-selling grocery item, right behind Diet Coke.

So what did SnackWell's do next? You already know the answer to that question. Put its name on everything except the kitchen sink. Naturally, SnackWell's sales promptly plummeted.

The issue is clear. It's the difference between building brands and milking brands. Most managers want to milk. "How far can we extend the brand? Let's spend some serious research money and find out."

Sterling Drug was a big advertiser and a big buyer of research. Its big brand was Bayer aspirin, but aspirin was losing out to acetaminophen (Tylenol) and ibuprofen (Advil).

So Sterling launched a $116-million advertising and

Coca-Cola...	$1,784 million
Pepsi-Cola..	$1,695 million
Campbell's..	$1,185 million
Kraft..........	$936 million
Folgers........	$927 million
Diet Coke.....	$846 million
SnackWell's..	$810 million

At one point, SnackWell's became the seventh-largest-selling grocery brand. Today sales are a fraction of what they once were.

None of the five products in the Bayer Select line contained aspirin. Why would anyone buy a Bayer product that didn't contain aspirin? They wouldn't.

marketing program to introduce a selection of five "aspirin-free" products. The Bayer Select line included headache-pain relief, regular pain relief, nighttime pain relief, sinus-pain relief, and a menstrual relief formulation, all of which contained either acetaminophen or ibuprofen as the core ingredient.

Results were painful. The first year Bayer Select sold $26 million worth of pain relievers in a $2.5 billion market, or about 1 percent of the market. Even worse, the sales of regular Bayer aspirin kept falling at about 10 percent a year. Why buy Bayer aspirin if the manufacturer is telling you that its "select" products are better because they are "aspirin-free"?

Are consumers stupid or not?

Many manufacturers are their own worst enemies. What are line extensions like *light, clear, healthy,* and *fat-free* actually telling you? That the regular products are not good for you.

- Heinz Light ketchup? Don't you suppose this leads customers to draw the conclusion that ketchup is loaded with calories? (Today, salsa outsells ketchup. As night follows day, we are sure to see in the future a brand called Pace Light salsa.)

- Hellmann's Light mayonnaise? Same question.

- Campbell's Healthy Request soup? Regular soup is unhealthy?

- Crystal Pepsi? What is wrong with the color of regular Pepsi?

Should Evian launch Sulfate-Free Evian spring water? (Check the label, there are 10 mg of sulfates in a liter of regular Evian. There are probably people out there who would like a sulfate-free version of the brand.)

Let sleeping brands lie. Before you launch your next line extension, ask yourself what customers of your current brand will think when they see the line extension.

If the market is moving out from under you, stay where you are and launch a second brand. If it's not, stay where you are and continue building your brand.

11   THE LAW OF FELLOWSHIP

In order to build the category, a brand
should welcome other brands.

The best thing that ever
happened to Coca-Cola was
Pepsi-Cola. The competition
between the two brands
raised consumer awareness
of the cola category.
Currently Coke and Pepsi
are the two largest-selling
grocery brands.

Greed often gets in the way of common sense. The dominant brand in a category often tries to broaden its appeal in
order to capture every last bit of market share.

"If we served beer and wine," the CEO of McDonald's
once said, "we might eventually have 100 percent of the
food-service market."

Unlikely. The law of expansion suggests the opposite.
When you broaden your brand, you weaken it. Look what
happened when McDonald's tried to broaden its appeal to
the adult market with the Arch Deluxe sandwich. Its market
share fell, and ultimately it was forced to discontinue the
product.

Which brings us to the law of fellowship. Not only
should the dominant brand tolerate competitors, it should
welcome them. The best thing that happened to Coca-Cola
was Pepsi-Cola. (To that end it's ironic that the Coca-Cola
Company fought Pepsi-Cola in the courts over the use of
"Cola" in its name. Fortunately for Coke, it lost, creating a
category which has been growing like gang busters ever
since.)

Choice stimulates demand. The competition between
Coke and Pepsi makes customers more cola conscious. Per
capita cola consumption goes up.

Remember, customers have choices, even when there is no competition. They can choose to drink beer, water, ginger ale, or orange juice instead of a cola. Competition increases the noise level and tends to increase sales in the category.

Competition also broadens the category while allowing the brands to stay focused. If Coca-Cola appeals to older people and Pepsi-Cola to younger people, the two brands can stay focused (and powerful) while at the same time broadening the market.

Customers respond to competition because choice is seen as a major benefit. If there is no choice, customers are suspicious. Maybe the category has some flaws? Maybe the price is too high? Who wants to buy a brand if you don't have another brand to compare it with?

You seldom see a big, growing, dynamic market without several major brands. Take the office superstore market. There are three big brands competing tooth and nail for this market: Office Depot, Office Max, and Staples.

So effective has this competition been that the number of independent office stationery stores has declined from about 10,000 in the past decade to 3,000 stores today.

Instead of welcoming competition, companies often feel threatened because they believe that future market shares will be based on the merits of the individual brands. An even playing field is not what most companies want. They want an unfair advantage, a playing field tilted to their side. Therefore, they think, let's try to drive out competitors before they get too established.

In the process, however, they fall victim to the laws of branding. Expansion, line extensions, and other strategies that broaden a brand's appeal will ultimately weaken the brand.

Market share is not based on merit, but on the power of the brand in the mind. In the long run, a brand is not necessarily a higher-quality product, but a higher-quality name.

Of course, customers can have too much choice. The

The proposed 1996 merger between Staples and Office Depot was blocked by the feds. It's too bad. Only two major brands are needed to create a dynamic market. The third brand is often superfluous.

In the long run, every category seems to be dominated by two major brands. In mouthwash it's Listerine and Scope.

more brands, the more flavors, the more varieties, the more confusion in the category. And the lower the per capita consumption.

For each category, two major brands seem to be ideal. Coca-Cola and Pepsi-Cola in cola, for example. Listerine and Scope in mouthwash. Kodak and Fuji in photographic film. Nintendo and PlayStation in video games. Duracell and Energizer in appliance batteries.

When there is too much choice, consumption suffers. Take wine, for example. In California alone, there are more than 1,000 wineries and 5,000 brands. *Wine Spectator* magazine publishes an annual issue with rankings of some 24,000 individual wines. (If you drank a bottle a day, it would take you more than sixty-five years to run through the lot. Then you would probably be too old to remember which wine you liked the best.)

With all that choice, you might think that Americans drink a lot of wine. But we don't. The per capita consumption of wine in the United States is one tenth that of France and one ninth that of Italy. Even the average German drinks three and a half times as much wine as the average American.

With so many small vineyards, so many different varieties, and a handful of connoisseurs with individual opinions about taste, the wine industry has yet to see the rise of any major brand. "That's just the way wine is," say industry experts. "Wine needs multiple brands, multiple vintages, multiple varieties." The motto seems to be "every acre its own brand."

That might be the law of wine, but it's not the law of branding. One day some company will do in wine what Absolut did in vodka and Jack Daniel's did in whiskey: build a big, powerful, worldwide brand.

You can also see the law of fellowship at work in the retail arena. Where one store may not make it, several stores will. Instead of being spread out in every section of a city, used-car dealers are often clustered along "automotive row." Where one dealer might have had trouble surviving, a handful of dealers are prospering. That's the power of fellowship.

In any large city, you can see the law of fellowship in action. Similar businesses tend to congregate in the same neighborhood. In New York City, for example, you will find the garment district on Seventh Avenue, the financial district on Wall Street, the diamond district on Forty-seventh Street, advertising agencies on Madison Avenue, theaters on Broadway, theme restaurants on West Fifty-seventh Street, and art galleries in SoHo.

It makes sense for similar businesses to be located close together. First, a group of similar businesses attract more customers to an area because there is more than one store to shop at. Second, customers can easily comparison shop among stores. Customers feel that without competition, companies may take advantage of them and rip them off. (The airlines have a reputation for doing this.) Third, having the competition nearby allows companies to keep an eye on each other. Companies are always anxious to keep track of trends in their industries.

Planet Hollywood discovered that one of the best locations in a city for its restaurant was across the street from its arch rival, Hard Rock Cafe. People attracted to this type of theme restaurant are already drawn to the area thanks to Hard Rock and can be enticed to eat at a Planet Hollywood across the street. Similarly, the best location for a Burger King franchise is often across the street from a McDonald's restaurant.

Take Branson, Missouri, which bills itself as the "music show capital of the world." Where one music theater in a town of 3,706 people might be hard-pressed to make ends meet, forty music theaters are well and prospering. It's the power of fellowship.

Your brand should welcome healthy competition. It often brings more customers into the category.

The best location for a Planet Hollywood is often across the street from a Hard Rock Cafe. This creates a "destination" that attracts more people than either theme restaurant could attract on its own.

And remember, no brand can ever own the entire market (unless of course it is a government-sanctioned monopoly).

Realistically, how much market share can the dominant brand achieve? Our research indicates that 50 percent is about the upper limit.

Federal Express has a 45 percent share of the domestic overnight package delivery market. Coca-Cola has a 50 percent share of the domestic cola market. For market shares higher than 50 percent, you need to consider launching multiple brands. Not just line extensions, but separate individual brands. (See Chapter 15, "The Law of Siblings.")

12   THE LAW OF THE GENERIC

One of the fastest routes to failure
is giving a brand a generic name.

History often leads us astray. In the past, some of the most successful companies (and brands) had generic names.

- General Motors, General Electric, General Mills, General Foods, General Dynamics.

- Standard Oil, Standard Brands, Standard Register Company, Standard Products Company.

- American Airlines, American Motors, American Broadcasting Company, American Telephone & Telegraph, American Express, Aluminum Company of America.

- National Broadcasting Company, National Biscuit Company, National Car Rental.

- International Business Machines, International Paper, International Harvester, International Nickel.

Some companies have even tried to combine two or more of these lofty "all things to all people" names. The American General Life and Accident Insurance Company, for example. (We're surprised that nobody thought to use "International General American Standard Products Company.")

In the past, companies thought they needed big, scopy,

Many local retail stores use generic names, which forever condemns them to be local retail stores. Virtually all the big national chains have proper names: McDonald's; Sears, Roebuck; Wal-Mart; Exxon; etc.

generic names. And the brand name was almost always the company name. (Today such an approach might produce the General Global Corp.) And yet, this naming strategy clearly worked. Why?

Years ago the market was flooded with commodities produced by thousands of small companies operating in a single town or region. The big, scopy, generic names put these small competitors in their place.

Many of these General, Standard, American, National, and International companies are still operating (and are still successful) today. Some of them are among the largest and best-known brands in the world.

The fact is, these brands/companies are successful in spite of their names.

We believe the primary reason for these corporate successes is the strategy and not the name.

- National Biscuit Company was the first national biscuit company.

- General Electric was the first general electric company.

- International Harvester was the first international harvester company.

Being first in the marketplace gave these companies such a head start and such a powerful presence in the market that it overcame the liability of their generic names.

Witness the shift from generic (or general) names to specific names: Nabisco, Alcoa, NBC, GE, ABC, IBM.

There are many national biscuit companies, but only one Nabisco. There are many aluminum companies in America, but only one Alcoa. There are many national broadcasting companies, but only one NBC.

Of course, we're sure that NBC always considered itself the National Broadcasting Company rather than a "national broadcasting company."

We don't generally like initials, but GE is a brand name and is therefore superior to General Electric, which is a generic name.

And therein lies the biggest mistake made when picking brand names. The process proceeds visually rather than verbally.

Executives often pass around the boardroom logotypes of prospective brand names, set in type and mounted on foamcore.

But the vast majority of brand communication takes place verbally, not visually. The average person spends nine times as much time listening to radio and television than he or she does reading magazines and newspapers.

Furthermore, in order to give meaning to the printed word, the mind processes sounds. The printed word is secondary to the sound that it generates in the reader's mind. So how can a reader differentiate the sound of the word "general" from the word "General"? With great difficulty.

The problem with a generic brand name is its inability to differentiate the brand from the competition. In the food supplement field, for example, a brand called Nature's Resource is spending $5 million a year to break into this growing market.

On the shelves of your local GNC store you'll also find the following products:

- Nature's Answer
- Nature's Best
- Nature's Bounty
- Nature's Gate
- Nature's Herb
- Nature's Plus
- Nature's Secret
- Nature's Sunshine Products
- Nature's Way
- Nature's Works

Will any of these generic brands break into the mind and become a major brand? Unlikely.

Even the legendary Lee Iacocca, father of the Mustang and former CEO of Chrysler Corporation (two powerful name brands), took the generic road when he launched his

What is Seattle's Best Coffee? Most people would probably answer, "Starbucks." It's hard for a generic name like Seattle's Best Coffee to register in the mind as a brand name.

own company, EV Global Motors. EV, for electric vehicle, is introducing a $995 electric bicycle. We can't see customers asking for an "EV Global bike."

What about a brand name, Lee? Like Schwinn or Trek or Cannondale?

The high-tech field is loaded with generic names that are unlikely to generate much in the way of brand identity. Security Software Systems, Power and Data Technology, Server Technology. Compare those names to Microsoft, Dell, and Intel, and you can see the power of a brand name over a generic name.

McAfee Associates, the leading maker of antivirus software, recently bought Network General for $1.3 billion. Guess what it chose for a new name?

It dropped McAfee, the only "name name" it owned in favor of two generics: Network Associates. It knew it had a name problem so it spent $10 million on the company's first television campaign, including more than a million for a Super Bowl spot.

As those thirty seconds flew by, did the viewer hear the words "network associates" or "Network Associates"? Generic names disappear into the ether. Only brand names register in the mind.

Just for Men hair coloring is also spending a fortune trying to build its brand. After watching a television commercial, the gray haired-man might think to himself, "What is the name of that hair-coloring product that's just for men?"

Nobody is saying that you should always invent a new name for an established brand, although that's often a good strategy for a product or service that is truly revolutionary and unlikely to be copied for some time. Kodak and Xerox are the usual suspects.

What you should generally do is take a regular word and use it out of context to connote the primary attribute of your brand.

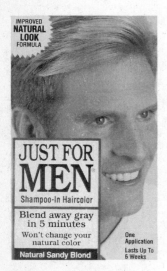

Is this shampoo-in hair color just for men, or is it Just For Men? When you listen to a television commercial, you're not sure. It's difficult to make a brand name out of a generic concept like "just for men."

Blockbuster Video is a powerful brand name. General Video Rental is not.

Hollywood brags about its "blockbusters," so Blockbuster Video borrowed the term to suggest it rents the best movies.

Budget is a powerful brand name for a car-rental service. The word suggests that it rents cars at low prices. Low-Cost Car Rental is not a good brand name.

Service Merchandise is a $4 billion company with a General Video name. It's too bad. The company's concept is compelling, but its generic name dooms the brand to relative obscurity.

Even though Service Merchandise is a big national retailer, it has low brand awareness because of its generic name. Recently the company went bankrupt.

The Luxury Car Company would have gone nowhere, in our opinion. But Toyota took the word "luxury," tweaked a few letters, and came up with Lexus, a superb brand name for a Japanese luxury car.

Some genius took the name of a specific office product and used it out of context to come up with Staples, an effective brand name for an office-supplies company. The double entendre is particularly powerful. "Buy your office staples from Staples."

Sometimes you can carve out a brand name by cutting a generic in half. This often has the further advantage of creating a short, distinctive, easy-to-remember brand name. Intelligent Chip Company is a lousy brand name, but Intel Corp. is terrific.

"Intelligent Chip inside" is a lousy advertising slogan. All computers have intelligent chips inside, but only the top-of-the-line products have "Intel inside."

One reason that line extensions fare so poorly in the marketplace is that they generally combine a brand name with a generic name. The weak generic name fails to create the separate identity that is the essence of the branding process. "Michelob Light" is perceived in the mind as "Michelob light," a watered-down version of the regular beer.

We're sure that Anheuser-Busch considers Michelob Light to be a brand name, but the consumer sees the "Light" as a generic name. In other words, Michelob Light is just a watered-down version of its regular beer.

The mind doesn't deal in letters or words. It deals in sounds. You can capitalize all you want, but a generic word is a generic word in the mind, no matter how you spell it.

Sometimes a company gets lucky. The line extension Vaseline Intensive Care skin lotion became the number-one hand lotion brand because the customer inadvertently treated Intensive Care as a brand name, not a descriptive generic name.

How do we know this to be true? Because customers call the product Intensive Care. "Hand me the Intensive Care."

Customers don't say, "Hand me the Vaseline." Unless, of course, they want the Vaseline.

On the other hand, if Vaseline had followed conventional line-extension thinking, it would have called the brand Vaseline Heavy-Duty skin lotion. "Hand me the Heavy Duty" is not something people are likely to say. "Heavy duty" is a generic term.

So why didn't Chesebrough-Pond's just call the brand Intensive Care in the first place? Good question and good thinking. You're ready for the next law.

13 THE LAW OF THE COMPANY

Brands are brands. Companies are companies. There is a difference.

Nothing causes as much confusion in the branding process as the proper use of a company name.

- Should the company name dominate the brand name? For example: Microsoft dominates Microsoft Word.

- Should the brand name dominate the company name? For example: Tide dominates Procter & Gamble.

- Or should they be given equal weight? For example: Gillette Sensor.

The issue of how to use a company name is at the same time simple and complicated. Simple, because the laws are so clear-cut. Complicated, because most companies do not follow the simple laws of branding and end up with a system that defies logic and results in endless brand-versus-company debates.

Brand names should almost always take precedence over company names. Consumers buy brands, they don't buy companies. So when a company name is used alone as a brand name (GE, Coca-Cola, IBM, Xerox, Intel), customers see these names as brands.

The best way to avoid confusion between a company name and a brand name is to use the company name in small type and the brand name in large type. The brand name is obviously "Mach 3," a product brought to you by a company called "Gillette."

Does the Tide brand need the corporate endorsement of the company name, Procter & Gamble? Probably not. Will a corporate endorsement hurt the brand? Probably not. Corporate endorsements are primarily for the trade, not for the enlightenment of the consumer.

When you combine a company name with a brand name in a clear and consistent fashion, the brand name is the primary name and the company name is seen as the secondary name: General Motors Cadillac.

Simple observation will demonstrate how seldom customers will use a company name . . . when they have been given a viable brand name to use. "How do you like my new Cadillac?"

Nobody says, "How do you like my new General Motors luxury car?"

With this caveat in mind, a company is a company as long as the name is not being used as a brand. A brand is a brand. There is a difference. A company is the organization that manufactures or produces the brand. It is not the brand itself. Microsoft isn't Word, Procter & Gamble isn't Tide. Microsoft produces many products, one of which is Word. Procter & Gamble produces many products, one of which is Tide.

While this makes sense, it's not usually the best branding strategy. Unless there are compelling reasons to do otherwise, the best branding strategy should be to use the company name as the brand name.

The WD-40 Company produces the WD-40 brand. The Zippo Corporation produces the Zippo brand. The Coca-Cola Company produces the Coca-Cola brand. Neat, simple, straightforward, easy to understand.

1. What's a Coca-Cola?

2. What's a Zippo?

3. What's a WD-40?

When you are a customer or prospect, the instant answers that come to mind are:

1. Cola. 2. Windproof lighter. 3. Lubricating spray.

When you are an employee of Coca-Cola, Zippo, or WD-40, on the other hand, the answer is usually different. It's the name on the paycheck. It's "my company."

Managers are employees, too. That's why management is company-oriented. And customers are brand-oriented.

Does the consumer care whether Toyota, Honda, or Nissan makes the Lexus? Probably not. But the president of Toyota USA certainly cares.

Does the customer care whether Nabisco or Kraft or Keebler makes Oreo cookies? Probably not. But the Nabisco marketing manager handling the Oreo brand certainly does.

Do you really care whether the publisher of this book was HarperBusiness, Simon & Schuster, or McGraw-Hill? (Do you even know without looking at the spine?)

But David Conti does. (He is our editor at HarperBusiness. And a good one, too.)

The view from the inside is totally different than the view from the outside. Managers must constantly remind themselves that customers care only about brands, not about companies.

It goes deeper than that. The brand isn't just the name the manufacturer puts on the package. It's the product itself. To a customer, Coca-Cola is, first and foremost, a dark, sweet, reddish-brown liquid. The brand name is the word customers use to describe that liquid. What's inside the bottle is the most important aspect of the branding process. Coca-Cola is branding the liquid itself.

It's not a cola made by the Coca-Cola Company. The cola itself is Coca-Cola, the real thing. This distinction is at the heart of an effective branding strategy.

A company that truly understands branding from the customer's point of view would have never introduced a product called "New Coke." How can you have a new, presumably better Coke? How can the real thing have been bad? Why on earth would you ever change it? It's like introducing New God.

Who makes Orville Redenbacher's gourmet popping corn? Does the customer really care? The power lies in the brand name, not in the company name.

In the same way, Rolex is not the brand name of an expensive sports watch made by the Rolex Watch Company Ltd. A Rolex is what you wrap around your wrist.

- Pop-Tarts are what you put in the toaster.

- Band-Aids are what you put on cuts.

- Tylenol is what you take for headaches.

Most issues involving company names versus brand names can be solved by asking yourself two questions:

1. What is the name of the brand?

2. What is the name of the stuff inside the packaging?

Both names had better be the same or you have big problems.

Let's explore what happens when you use both the company name and the brand name on the package. Let's look at Microsoft Excel.

The "Microsoft" part of the name is redundant. Nobody but Microsoft makes Excel software. Since customers tend to simplify names as much as possible, Microsoft Excel quickly becomes Excel. "Let's buy Excel."

Microsoft Word is another matter. "Word" is a generic word. Furthermore, many of Microsoft's competitors have used "word" in their product names. WordPerfect, Word-Star, etc. As a result, customers tend to use the full name of the product, "Microsoft Word." This is not necessarily good from the company's point of view. As a general rule, you want your brand name to be as short and as memorable as possible. (Short names greatly improve your word-of-mouth possibilities.)

When customers feel they have to use both your company

name and your brand name together, you usually have a branding problem. (Normally because you used a generic word for your brand name.) Take Campbell's Chunky soup, for example.

Is the product Chunky soup or chunky soup? Customers can't be sure, so they ask for Campbell's Chunky soup. Campbell should have used a different brand name.

Take the Sony Trinitron. Is trinitron a type of cathode-ray tube or is Trinitron a brand name for a television set? Customers aren't sure, so they ask for a Sony Trinitron.

As far as the customer is concerned, the easiest, simplest way is the Procter & Gamble way. Use just the brand name boldly on the package and relegate "The Procter & Gamble Company" to tiny type at the bottom. That's how the company name is handled on Bold, Cheer, Ivory, Tide, etc.

But a case can be made for the middle way. Some of today's more sophisticated, discriminating customers might like to know who makes a particular brand. They won't, however, use both names together. Nobody calls an Acura a "Honda Acura." Or a Lincoln a "Ford Lincoln."

Furthermore, there is often interest in the trade (which includes retailers and distributors) about the company behind a brand. For example, whom do we order Tide from?

For many brands one answer is to put the company name in small type above the brand name. Customers who are strongly motivated to use only the brand name will hardly notice the company name. Yet the trade and today's more sophisticated customers will be able to easily find the name of the company behind the brand.

The danger, of course, lies inside the corporation. With this branding strategy, you tend to get inundated with suggestions like, "Why can't we make the corporate name larger? We're wasting all these opportunities to promote our stock, improve employee relationships, build a better relationship with the trade." (On second thought, maybe you should leave the company name off the package entirely.)

You can't force a brand name into a mind. Campbell's has tried to make Chunky the brand name for its Chunky soup and Campbell's the company name. But the prospect sees Chunky as a generic name and the brand as Campbell's.

Sony has succeeded in making PlayStation the name of the video-game brand brought to you by Sony.

This is confusing. Is the name of the brand Gillette or Trac II?

Look what happened at Gillette. Both the Trac II and the Atra razors were marketed with the company name the same size as the brand names.

Not a good idea. The brand name should dominate the company name.

With the Mach 3, Gillette has returned to basics. The Mach 3 name dominates.

No issue in branding is so thoroughly discussed as the proper role and function of the company name. And yet, in most cases, it's a nonissue.

The brand itself should be the focus of your attention. If you have to use the company name, use it. But do so in a decidedly secondary way.

14   THE LAW OF SUBBRANDS

What branding builds, subbranding
can destroy.

Management tends to invent terminology in order to give
legitimacy to the branding moves it wants to make.

- Holiday Inn, the leading hotel/motel operator, wanted to
  get into the upscale hotel segment.
- Cadillac, the leading upscale domestic automobile brand,
  wanted to introduce a smaller car.
- Waterford, the leading Irish crystal maker, wanted to
  market a less expensive line.
- Donna Karan, a top designer, wanted to market less costly
  and more casual clothes.

Typical line-extension strategies would have produced
brand names like Holiday Inn Deluxe, Cadillac Light, Budget Waterford, and Kasual Karan. Even the most callow
marketing people would have found these brand names difficult to swallow.

What to do? Invent a subbrand. So we have Holiday Inn
Crowne Plaza, Cadillac Catera, Marquis by Waterford, and
DKNY. Now we can have our cake and eat it, too. We can use
our well-known core brand at the same time as we launch secondary or subbrands to move into new territory.

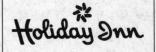

Holiday Inn has become a
megabrand with the launch
of subbrands like Holiday
Inn Express, Holiday Inn
Select, Holiday Inn
SunSpree Resorts, and
Holiday Inn Garden Court.
This subbranding is eroding
the power of the core brand.

After twenty years of trying to establish a brand called Holiday Inn Crowne Plaza, the company finally gave up and now calls its upscale hotel chain just "Crowne Plaza."

But what sounds right in the boardroom often doesn't make sense in the marketplace.

- Did anybody ever walk into a Holiday Inn and ask the clerk at the front desk: "Don't you have a more expensive hotel I can stay at?"

- Did anybody ever walk into a Cadillac dealership and ask: "Don't you have any smaller Cadillacs?" (Bigger maybe, but not smaller.)

- Did anybody ever walk into Bloomingdale's and ask the salesperson: "Don't you have any cheap Waterford?"

- Did anybody ever walk into a Donna Karan showroom and ask: "The suits are lovely, but where can I buy her sweatpants?"

The marketing world is awash in conceptual thinking that has no relationship to the real world. Subbranding is one of those concepts.

Customer research at Holiday Inn Crowne Plaza produced what you might have expected: "It's a nice hotel, but it's a little expensive for a Holiday Inn." The company finally got the message and is in the process of cutting the megabrand connection. From now on, the hotels will be known as Crowne Plaza, period.

A Cadillac dealership is the last place in the world where you would look for a small car. First they tried Cimarron, which went nowhere and was eventually dropped. Naturally, Cadillac didn't give up. Its latest small-car incarnation is called the Cadillac Catera.

On the other hand, Marquis by Waterford is a big success, but partially at the expense of the high-priced line. You have to wonder if there is a Gresham's law of marketing, too. Sooner or later, we expect the Marquis line to seriously erode the regular Waterford product.

Donna Karan has gone off in way too many directions. In addition to the basic line, there is Donna Karan menswear, DKNY, DKNY menswear, and DKNY kids. The company has also gotten into intimate apparel and beauty products. Recently, the company sold out to LVMH.

Customers have a cornucopia of choice. Subbranders assume otherwise. Why would a customer expect Holiday Inn to have an upscale hotel? Wouldn't the customer more likely try Hilton, Hyatt, or Marriott first? Why spend all that money and still stay at a Holiday Inn! The thinking is, If I am forking out the big bucks, I want to stay with a top hotel brand.

Subbranding is an inside-out branding strategy that tries to push the core brand into new directions. It captures management's attention because of what it promises, not necessarily because of what it delivers.

In spite of the subbranding setback at Holiday Inn Crowne Plaza, the company has moved into Holiday Inn Express, Holiday Inn Select, Holiday Inn SunSpree Resorts, and Holiday Inn Garden Court.

You used to know exactly what you would find in a Holiday Inn. In fact, that was the theme of its long-running advertising campaign: "The best surprise is no surprise."

What's a Holiday Inn Select? Go ahead. Book a room and be surprised.

Subbranding has taken its share of criticism, so the marketing establishment is rethinking the concept. Leading-edge practitioners today are more likely to call the concept a masterbrand or megabrand strategy. It's especially prevalent in the automotive field.

"Ford is not our brand. Our brands are: Aspire, Contour, Crown Victoria, Escort, Mustang, Probe, Taurus, and Thunderbird." What's a Ford then? "A Ford is a megabrand."

"Dodge is not our brand. Our brands are: Avenger, Intrepid, Neon Stealth, Stratus, and Viper." What's a Dodge then? "A Dodge is a megabrand."

Holiday Inn Express has one of the most memorable television advertising campaigns. ("I'm not an orthopedic surgeon, but I stayed at a Holiday Inn Express last night.") But what's a Holiday Inn Express and how does it differ from a Holiday Inn Select? Who knows.

Many automobile companies make a serious error by promoting just their model names on the most road-visible part of their cars, the rear end. If you see a good-looking car called an STS in front of you, where do you go to buy one? (Hint: The Seville STS is made by the Cadillac Division of General Motors.)

You can't apply your own branding system to a market that sees things differently. What the manufacturer sees as a brand, the customer sees as a model. What the manufacturer sees as a megabrand, the customer sees as a brand. (Customers don't understand the megabrand concept at all.)

Even Keith Crain, publisher of *Automotive News*, the industry's bible, is dubious of what car-marketing people are trying to do. "A lot of folks out there tell you that individual models, not the nameplates, are the brands. I don't know of any models that have ads in the Yellow Pages."

Can a brand be marketed in more than one model? Sure, as long as those models don't detract from the essence of the brand, that singular idea or concept that sets it apart from all other brands.

When you feel the need to create subbrands, you are chasing the market, you are not building the brand.

The essence of a brand is some idea or attribute or market segment you can own in the mind. Subbranding is a concept that takes the brand in exactly the opposite direction. Subbranding destroys what branding builds.

Branding concepts that are not driven by the marketplace are going to go nowhere. Subbranding, masterbranding, and megabranding are not customer-driven concepts. They have no meaning in the minds of most consumers.

Think simple. Think like a customer and your brand will become more successful.

15 THE LAW OF SIBLINGS

There is a time and a place to
launch a second brand.

The laws of branding seem to suggest that a company concentrate all of its resources on a single brand for a single market. Keep the brand focused and ignore opportunities to get into new territories.

True. But there comes a time when a company should launch a second brand. And perhaps a third, even a fourth brand.

A second-brand strategy is not for every company. If handled incorrectly, the second brand can dilute the power of the first brand and waste resources.

Yet, in some situations, a family of brands can be developed that will assure a company's control of a market for many decades to come.

Take the Wm. Wrigley Jr. Company. For more than a hundred years, Wrigley has dominated the chewing gum market, generating billions of dollars of profits. But not with one brand. Today Wrigley has a family of brands.

Wrigley's dominates the chewing gum market with seven major brands.

- Big Red (a cinnamon-flavored brand)
- Doublemint (a peppermint-flavored brand)
- Extra (a sugar-free brand)
- Freedent (a stick-free brand)

- Juicy Fruit (a fruit-flavored brand)

- Spearmint (a spearmint-flavored brand)

- Winterfresh (a breath-freshener brand)

The key to a family approach is to make each sibling a unique individual brand with its own identity. Resist the urge to give the brands a family look or a family identity. You want to make each brand as different and distinct as possible.

The Wrigley approach is not perfect. Wrigley's first three brands (Juicy Fruit, Spearmint, and Doublemint) are too much like line extensions. They need the Wrigley name to support their generic brand names. Big Red, Extra, Freedent, and Winterfresh, however, can stand on their own, each as totally separate brands.

Most managers are too internally focused to see the power of a separate identity. They want to "take advantage of the equity" their brand already owns in the mind in order to successfully launch a new brand.

So IBM launches brands like the IBM PCjr. And NyQuil launches DayQuil. And Blockbuster Video launches Blockbuster Music. And Toys "R" Us launches Babies "R" Us.

Time Inc. became the world's largest magazine publisher, not by launching line extensions of its core brand, but by launching totally separate publications. Like Wrigley, Time Inc. has seven publishing powerhouses.

1. *Time*

2. *Fortune* (not *Time for Business*)

3. *Life* (not *Time for Pictures*)

4. *Sports Illustrated* (not *Time for Sports*)

5. *Money* (not *Time for Finances*)

6. *People* (not *Time for Celebrities*)

7. *Entertainment Weekly* (not *Time for Entertainment*)

Bring an IBM PCjr home for the holidays.

Why would anyone in his right mind call a computer product for the home an IBM PCjr? What marketing needs more than anything else is a dose of common sense.

(Nobody's perfect. So now we also have *Digital Time*, *Teen People*, and *Sports Illustrated for Kids*.)

And what about *ESPN Magazine*? Does anyone except Disney really believe that *ESPN Magazine* will score any goals against *Sports Illustrated*? We certainly don't. The strength of a brand lies in having a separate, unique identity—not in being associated in the mind with a totally different category.

Having a totally separate identity in the mind doesn't mean creating a totally separate organization to handle each brand. Wm. Wrigley Jr. Company doesn't have seven separate manufacturing plants or seven separate sales organizations. It has seven brands and one company, one sales force, one marketing organization.

When General Mills decided to get into the Italian restaurant business, it didn't start from scratch. It used everything it had learned about the seafood restaurant business to jump-start its Italian sibling. The one thing it did not do was to spin off its Red Lobster name. No Italian Red Lobsters.

General Mills invented a separate brand called Olive Garden. With this strategy, the company was able to create the two largest family-restaurant chains in America. (Subsequently, the two chains were spun off into Darden Restaurants, Inc., which immediately became the world's largest casual-dining company.)

When Sara Lee tried to take its panty hose brand into the supermarket trade, it didn't use its Hanes name. Nor did it call the new brand Hanes II or Hanes Too.

Sara Lee created a separate brand designed for supermarket distribution called L'eggs. Packaged in a plastic egg, the product became the number-one supermarket brand and the number-one panty hose brand, with 25 percent of the total panty hose market.

When Black & Decker, the world's largest power-tool manufacturer, wanted to get into the professional power-

General Mills launched the Red Lobster chain, which became a big success, the largest family restaurant chain in America.

When General Mills decided to launch a chain featuring Italian foods, it did so with a totally different name, Olive Garden.

Designing a brand for a distribution channel can be an extremely effective strategy. Everything about the L'eggs brand, including the name and the packaging, was designed for supermarket distribution.

When Honda wanted to introduce an expensive car, it didn't call the brand a Honda Plus or a Honda Ultra. It developed a new brand called Acura, which became a big success. As a matter of fact, Acura quickly became the largest-selling imported luxury car in America.

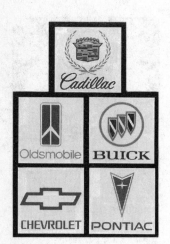

General Motors was most successful when it kept each of its brands separate, with little or no overlap between divisions.

tool market, it didn't use the Black & Decker name. Nor did it call the new product Black & Decker Pro.

Black & Decker created a separate brand called DeWalt. In less than three years, DeWalt became a $350 million business, the market leader in professional tools, and the second-largest power-tool brand after Black & Decker.

In the past, companies have created families of brands based on the principles behind the law of siblings. As time goes by, they forget why the brands were created in the first place. Instead of maintaining separate identities, the brands are mashed together and a layer of corporate frosting added on top. Instead of becoming stronger, the brands become weaker.

General Motors used to market a phalanx of five brands, each with its own identity. Chevrolet, Pontiac, Oldsmobile, Buick, and Cadillac. Any twelve-year-old kid could spot a Chevy a block away and instantly identify the brand. Or a Pontiac. Or an Oldsmobile. Or a Buick. Or a Cadillac.

Holes in the front fender? That's a Buick. Fins on the back fenders? That's a Cadillac.

No more. Even if you work for General Motors, we defy you to spot GM cars on the street and then correctly identify the brands.

Many CEOs believe that a sibling strategy works best when the organization itself is decentralized. "Let the brands fight it out among themselves."

Not so. That belief is what got General Motors in trouble. Control over the brands (or divisions) was lifted and each division allowed to set its own course. Results were predictable. Each division broadened the scope of its brand and the world ended up with expensive Chevrolets, cheap Cadillacs, and bewildering brand confusion.

A sibling strategy requires more top-management supervision, not less. The urgent, long-term need is to maintain the separation between the brands, not to make them all alike. Human instincts work in the opposite direction. Result: All General Motors cars ended up with fins.

THE LAW OF SIBLINGS

Nor is there a need to tag the corporate identity on every brand. Does the customer buy a Lexus because it's made by Toyota? Or in spite of the fact that it's made by Toyota?

The customer buys a Lexus. That's the power of the Lexus brand. The corporate connection is irrelevant.

In particular, corporate management should keep the following principles in mind when selecting a sibling strategy for its stable of brands.

Who makes the Lexus? Lexus owners don't like to be reminded that a Lexus is made by Toyota, which is why Toyota wisely keeps its name off the vehicle.

1. Focus on a common product area. Passenger cars, chewing gum, over-the-counter drugs, these are some common product areas around which to build a sibling portfolio.

2. Select a single attribute to segment. Price is the most common, but other attributes include distribution, age, calories, sex, flavors. By segmenting a single attribute only, you reduce the potential confusion between your brands. What you want to avoid is any overlap among brands. Keep each brand unique and special.

3. Set up rigid distinctions among brands. Price is the easiest attribute to segment because you can put specific numbers on each brand. When prices overlap, it's very difficult to keep the brands separate. Most car owners confused Oldsmobile and Buick because their price ranges were quite similar.

4. Create different, not similar brand names. You don't want to create a family of brands, you want to create a family of different brands. Look at some of Chevrolet's model names: Cavalier, Camaro, Corsica, Caprice, Corvette. (Recently they dropped Corsica and Caprice, but those "C" names are still confusing.)

    One reason these model names can't be brands is the fact that they are too similar. If Chevrolet wanted to create brands instead of model names, it should have used distinctive names. Alliteration is the curse of a sibling family.

5. Launch a new sibling only when you can create a new category. New brands should not be launched just to fill a hole in the line or to compete directly with an existing competitor. This principle is the one most often violated by even the largest of companies. Coca-Cola launched Mr. Pibb, not to create a new category, but to block the growth of Dr Pepper. Coca-Cola launched Fruitopia, not to create a new category, but to block the growth of Snapple. Then they launched Mello Yello to block the growth of Mountain Dew. That didn't work, so they launched Surge, which didn't work either. All four brands have gone nowhere.

6. Keep control of the sibling family at the highest level. If you don't, you will find that your powerful, distinctive brands will slowly fall apart. They will become victims of sibling rivalry, a pattern of corporate behavior that depends upon copying the best features of a brand's sibling competitors. You'll end up like General Motors with a family of brands that all look alike.

A family of sibling brands is not a strategy for every corporation. But where it is appropriate, a sibling strategy can be used to dominate a category over the long term.

16

THE LAW OF SHAPE

A brand's logotype should be designed
to fit the eyes. Both eyes.

A logotype is a combination of a trademark, which is a visual symbol of the brand, and the name of the brand set in distinctive type.

Logotypes come in all shapes. Round, square, oval, horizontal, vertical. But all shapes are not created equal in the eyes of the consumer.

Since the eyes of your customers are mounted side by side, the ideal shape for a logotype is horizontal. Roughly two and one-fourth units wide and one unit high.

This horizontal shape will provide the maximum impact for your logotype. This is true wherever the logotype is used: on buildings, brochures, letterheads, advertisements, or calling cards.

This horizontal bias is especially important when a logotype is used on a retail establishment. In the neon jungle, a vertical logotype is at a severe disadvantage. The Arby's cowboy-hat logo is an example of the penalty of verticality.

Of equal importance to shape is legibility. Logotype designers often go way overboard in picking a typeface to express the attribute of a brand rather than its ability to be clearly read.

Typefaces come in thousands of styles and weights, but customers are only dimly aware of the differences. To para-

A customer sees the world through two horizontally mounted eyes peering out of his or her head. It's like looking out the windshield of an automobile. For maximum visual impact, a logotype should have the same shape as a windshield, roughly two and one-fourth units wide and one unit high. The Avis logotype is almost the perfect shape. The Arby's logotype is much too vertical.

FENDI
HERMÈS
ChristianDior
LANCÔME
RALPH LAUREN
ESCADA
GUERLAIN

Many of the world's most famous brands use simple typography in their logotypes. The power of a brand resides in the name, not in the typeface.

Legibility is the most important aspect of a typeface. This Lord & Taylor logotype is almost unreadable.

phrase David Ogilvy, no woman says, I would have bought that detergent except they had to go and set the headline in Futura Demibold.

What typeface does Rolex use in its logotype? Ralph Lauren? Rolls-Royce? Serif or sans serif?

The truth is, the words (Rolex, Ralph Lauren, Rolls-Royce) are what communicate the power of the brands. The typefaces used in their logotypes can help or hinder the communication process, but only slightly.

On the other hand, if the typeface is virtually illegible, the logotype has little or no meaning in the consumer's mind. Not because of the typeface used, but because the prospect can't read the words. Legibility is the most important consideration in selecting a typeface used in a logotype.

Certainly, there are perceptual differences in the feelings that typefaces communicate. Sans serif typefaces look modern; serif typefaces look old-fashioned. Bold typefaces look masculine; light typefaces look feminine.

But these differences become obvious only by exaggeration. Would you really want to set your brand name in black-letter Gothic (the typeface used in the *New York Times* logotype) in order to make your brand look like an old, established brand? We think not. While it may make a visual impression, few prospects would be able to read (and therefore remember) the name.

It's a vicious cycle. In order to get the average prospect to notice the "mood" of the logotype you have to exaggerate the characteristics of the typography. And when you do that, you lose the logotype's legibility. It's not worth the trade-off.

The other component of the logotype, the trademark, or visual symbol, is also overrated. The meaning lies in the word, or words, not in the visual symbol.

It's the Nike name that gives meaning to the Swoosh symbol. The Swoosh symbol doesn't give much meaning to the Nike brand. After a symbol has been associated with a name for a long period of time, the symbol can represent the name, through a kind of "rebus" effect. But it's still the name that carries the brand's power.

So the Swoosh stands for Nike. But the advantages of using the symbol alone are slim and occur only in certain situations. Perhaps you can see the symbol at a distance where the name alone would be unreadable. Perhaps you can use the symbol on the product itself or on articles of clothing where the name would look too "commercial." Perhaps after spending hundreds of millions a year for over a decade to link the Swoosh to Nike, you can get away with ending your commercials with only the symbol. But what is the advantage in doing so?

Compare Shell with Mobil. Shell uses a shell trademark on its gasoline stations without the word "Shell." Mobil uses a logotype with blue letters and a red "O" to spell the word "Mobil."

Is the Shell approach superior to the Mobil approach? We think not. The best you can say is that the Shell approach works, thanks to a simple name and an easy-to-translate simple visual. But what are the advantages of the Shell approach?

Very few. And there are some disadvantages. As people grow up and new prospects come into the marketplace, how will they learn that the yellow symbol means "Shell"? Especially if the prospect doesn't know that Shell is a brand name for a gasoline.

A great deal of effort has gone into creating elaborate symbols for use in logotypes. Crests, shields, coats of arms, and other heraldic symbols have poured out of America's design shops in great profusion. For the most part, these efforts are wasted. The power of a brand name lies in the meaning of the word in the mind. For most brands, a symbol has little or nothing to do with creating this meaning in the mind.

There are only a handful of simple symbols that make effective trademarks. (The Mercedes three-pointed star is one of them.) At this late date, if history hasn't willed you one of these simple symbols, it's probably too late to create one on your own.

Mobil gasoline stations used to feature Pegasus, the flying red horse. By dropping the horse and designing a simple logotype with blue letters and a red O, Mobil greatly increased the visibility of its stations.

17

THE LAW OF COLOR

A brand should use a color that is the opposite of its major competitor's.

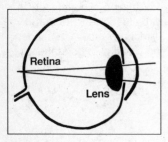

Because the eye focuses red light slightly behind the retina, red light appears to move toward you.

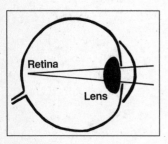

Because the eye focuses blue light slightly in front of the retina, blue light appears to move away from you.

Another way to make a brand distinctive is with color. But color is not an easy attribute to work with. There are thousands of words to choose from in order to create a unique name, but only a handful of colors.

There are five basic colors (red, orange, yellow, green, and blue) plus the neutral colors (black, white, and gray). It's best to stick to one of these five primary colors rather than an intermediate or mixed color. But which color?

Keep in mind that all colors are not created equal in the eye of the beholder. Colors on the red end of the spectrum are focused slightly behind the retinas in your eyes. Therefore, a red color appears to move toward your eyes while you're looking at it.

Colors on the blue end of the spectrum, on the other hand, are focused slightly in front of the retinas in your eyes. A blue color appears to move away from you.

Because of these physical reasons, red is the color of energy and excitement. Red is an in-your-face color. Which is why red is the dominant color in 45 percent of all national flags. (Blue is a distinct second. Blue dominates in less than 20 percent of all flags.)

Blue is the opposite of red. Blue is peaceful and tranquil. Blue is a laid-back color.

In the world of brands, red is a retail color used to attract attention. Blue is a corporate color used to communicate stability. For example, Coca-Cola red and IBM blue.

The other primary colors are in between. Orange is more like red than blue. Green is more like blue than red.

Yellow is the neutral color. But because it is in the middle of the range of wavelengths your eyes can detect, yellow is also the brightest color. (Its brightness is the reason yellow is often used to communicate "caution," as in yellow lights, yellow lines, yellow signs, etc.)

Over the years, some colors have become identified with various attributes, occasions, and movements.

- White is the color of purity (as in a white wedding gown).
- Black is the color of luxury (as in Johnnie Walker Black Label).
- Blue is the color of leadership (as in the blue ribbon award to the winner of a horse show).
- Purple is the color of royalty (as in the expression "born to the purple").
- Green is the color of the environment and health (as in Greenpeace, Healthy Choice, and SnackWell's).

When selecting a color for a brand or a logo, managers usually focus on the mood they want to establish rather than the unique identity they want to create. And while mood or tone can be important, other factors should override a choice based on mood alone.

Leaders have first choice. Normally the best color to select is the one that is most symbolic of the category. John Deere is the leading brand of farm tractor. Does it surprise you that John Deere picked green, the color of grass, trees, and agriculture, as the brand's signature color?

For a new Brazilian tractor, we picked the name "Maxion" because it symbolizes power. We also picked the color blue to differentiate Maxion from the two leading brands, which were green and red.

For a tractor company in Brazil, we were asked to develop a brand name and color. We picked the name Maxion as the brand name because it seemed to communicate "power," a key attribute in a farm tractor. But what color should this new tractor brand use?

John Deere used green. The second brand in the market used red. So the color choice was obvious. Maxion became a blue tractor and a blue brand.

Is blue a good color for a farm tractor? No, but it's more important to create a separate brand identity than it is to use the right symbolic color.

Hertz, the first car-rental brand, picked yellow. So Avis, the second brand, picked red. National went with green. (For years, National gave out S&H Green Stamps to car-rental customers, a marketing move that helped associate the National name with the color green.)

There is a powerful logic for selecting a color that is the opposite of your major competitors. When you ignore this law of color, you do so at your own risk.

Cola is a reddish-brown liquid, so the logical color for a cola brand is red. Which is one reason why Coca-Cola has been using red for more than a hundred years.

Pepsi-Cola made a poor choice. It picked red and blue as the brand's colors. Red to symbolize cola and blue to differentiate the brand from Coca-Cola. For years Pepsi has struggled with a less-than-ideal response to Coke's color strategy.

Be honest. In your mind's eye, doesn't the world seem to be awash in Coca-Cola signs? And isn't it hard to picture many Pepsi-Cola signs? Pepsi is out there, but the lack of a unique differentiating color tends to make Pepsi invisible in a sea of Coca-Cola red.

Recently Pepsi-Cola has seen the light, or rather the color. It is doing what it should have done more than fifty years ago. Make the brand's color the opposite of its major competitor's color.

Pepsi-Cola is going blue. Pepsi even went to the expense of painting a Concorde supersonic jet blue to carry the color message to bottlers around the world.

Be the opposite. Kodak is yellow, so Fuji is green.

Yellow (as in the Golden Arches) is also the color most identified with McDonald's, although the actual logotype is mostly red. But what color is Burger King?

Burger King made the mistake of symbolizing the colors of a hamburger rather than picking a color to contrast with the leader. Burger King combined the yellow of a hamburger bun with the orange-red of the meat. A neat logotype, but a lousy color choice.

Budweiser is red, so what color should Miller be?

One of the many problems with the massive line extensions marketed by Miller is that they destroy the brand's color identity. To differentiate the Miller line extensions from each other, the brand uses an array of color combinations. In the process Miller misses an opportunity to differentiate its core brand from Budweiser, its key competitor.

Think of the unmistakable color of a Tiffany box. By standardizing on a single color and using it consistently over the years, you can build a powerful visual presence in a clutter-filled world. At Christmastime, every brand and retail store uses green and red to celebrate the holiday, from M&M's to Macy's. Yet Tiffany & Co. sticks to blue, and becomes even more noticeable under the tree as a result.

Women hug their husbands as soon as they see the robin's-egg blue box—without opening it they know it will be wonderful.

You have probably seen many more Miller cans than Tiffany boxes, but we would bet that you know the hue of a Tiffany box and that you're not quite sure about Miller.

While a single color is almost always the best color strategy for a brand, sometimes you can make a case for multiple colors. Federal Express, the first overnight-package-

TIFFANY & CO.

What color is a Tiffany box? It's that distinctive robin's-egg blue. If Tiffany had used a variety of colors for its boxes, it would have lost a marvelous opportunity to reinforce the brand name with a distinctive color.

delivery company, wanted its packages to stand out on the recipient's desk. So it combined the two most shocking colors it could find: orange and purple.

When a FedEx package arrives, everybody can see that a FedEx package has arrived. It's like an orange-and-purple suit in a sea of corporate blue.

Color consistency over the long term can help a brand burn its way into the mind. Look at what yellow has done for Caterpillar, brown for United Parcel Service, red for Coca-Cola, the green jacket for the Masters golf tournament, and blue for IBM.

What blue did for Big Blue, a unique color can do for your big brand.

18   THE LAW OF BORDERS

There are no barriers to global branding.
A brand should know no borders.

In our consulting work we find that most clients strongly
believe two things:

1. Their brands' market shares cannot be substantially
   increased in their home countries.

2. They need to grow.

As a result of these ironclad beliefs, they insist on
expanding their brands into other categories. "It's the only
way to grow," they say.

So they fall victim to the first law of branding, the law of
expansion. "Sure," they say. "Expanding our line may be
dangerous, but it's the only way to grow."

It's not the only way to grow. In fact, the perfect solution to
achieving both goals is to build a global brand. That means:

• Keep the brand's narrow focus in its home country.

• Go global.

For years the magic word on many products has been
"imported." Food, beer, wine, liquor, clothing, automobiles,

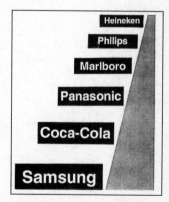

Heineken
Philips
Marlboro
Panasonic
Coca-Cola
Samsung

Fly into any major city in the
world, take a taxi downtown,
and look at the billboards.
What country are you in?
What continent are you on?
The world is in the process
of becoming one big global
marketplace.

Heineken NV exports its brand to some 170 different countries. In most of these countries Heineken is the largest-selling high-priced beer. (Today Heineken brews its beer locally in some fifty different countries.)

appliances, and many other items have benefited from an imported label. As if crossing a border suddenly increases the value of the brand.

Actually, crossing a border often does add value to a brand. Since value lies in the mind of the consumer, the perception of where the brand came from can add or subtract value. Does anyone doubt the value of:

- Watches from Switzerland

- Wines from France

- Automobiles from Germany

- Electronic products from Japan

- Clothing from Italy

Would watches from Albania, wine from Poland, cars from Turkey, electronic products from Russia, or clothing from Portugal have the same perceptions? Obviously not.

Every country has its own unique perceptions. When a brand is in sync with its own country's perceptions, that brand has the possibility of becoming a global brand.

Wherever you live in the world today, chances are high that a significant number of people are wearing Swiss watches, driving German cars, drinking French wines, playing with Japanese electronic products, and dressing in Italian clothes. (Hopefully, not all at the same time.)

In spite of duties, tariffs, import quotas, inspections, regulations, red tape, and petty harassments, the world is becoming one big global market. And your product had better get on the global brandwagon or risk losing out altogether.

Heineken NV is the leading brewery in the Netherlands, a small country with a population of only 15 million. Yet by going global Heineken NV has become the second-largest brewery in the world.

Can any brewery do the same? Of course not. To be successful as a worldwide beer brand (or any worldwide brand), you need to do two things:

1. You need to be first.

2. Your product needs to fit the perceptions of its country of origin.

Heineken was the first beer brand to pursue a global strategy. But beer is a product closely associated with Germany, not Holland.

Heineken got lucky. Holland is close to Germany, both geographically and ethnically. As a result, many beer drinkers think Heineken is a German product. (The company has been known to distribute cardboard coasters to bars and restaurants with the words "printed in Germany" featured on the coasters.)

Heineken also got lucky in a second way. Beck's, its major German competitor on the global market, is saddled with an English-sounding name.

Heineken got lucky in a third way. The largest-selling beer in Germany is Warsteiner. Normally, the leading brand in a country known for the category can be a big success in the rest of the world. (Witness the success of Barilla in the U.S. market with the theme "Italy's #1 pasta.") But no German beer brand starting with "War" is going to have much of a chance on the global beer market.

As the largest-selling beer in Germany, a country noted for beer, Warsteiner has a natural advantage. But it didn't move rapidly enough into the global market. Furthermore, the brand suffers from a weak name.

There are many ways to play the global game. Instead of appealing to the core market, you can appeal to a different segment of the market. Corona Extra has become a global force by associating the brand with the boom in Mexican cuisine. Asahi beer has done the same with Japanese cuisine. And Tsingtao beer with Chinese cuisine.

Corona Extra is a good example of the skillful use of a country's perception to promote a brand. Because a wedge of citrus was associated with the drinking of Mexican tequila, the importers of Corona Extra used the same imagery to launch the brand.

The toothpick and lime on top of the Corona bottle became a visual symbol that you could see halfway across a bar or restaurant. "What's that?" asked the non-Corona-drinking consumer.

"It's Corona Extra, the Mexican beer." So successful was this strategy that the brand became the largest-selling imported beer in the United States, topping even Heineken. In a twist, its American success has stimulated sales south of the border, where Corona Extra has become the leading beer brand in Mexico.

The perception of a country is important. There is no such thing as a global brand with a global perception.

- Toyota, Honda, and Nissan are global brands with Japanese perceptions.

- Compaq, Intel, and Microsoft are global brands with American perceptions.

- Dom Pérignon, Perrier-Jouët, and Château Mouton-Rothschild are global brands with French perceptions.

- Gucci, Versace, and Giorgio Armani are global brands with Italian perceptions.

With some 62 percent of its sales and 76 percent of its profits outside of North America, Coca-Cola insists that it is a global brand, not an American brand. And it is, literally. (Robert Goizueta, Coke's longtime chief executive, was from Cuba. Its current CEO, Douglas Daft, is from Australia.)

But it would be a major marketing mistake for Coca-Cola to abandon its American heritage. Every brand (no matter where it is bottled, assembled, manufactured, or produced) has to be from somewhere. As American culture (especially in music, film, and television) has permeated the

Even a global brand has to start somewhere. Coca-Cola is a global brand with an American identity.

world, Coca-Cola has benefited greatly because of its American connection. "It's the real thing," Coke drinkers will say proudly with accents from places far and wide.

Every brand, just like every person, is from somewhere. A fifth-generation Irish-American might say he or she is "Irish." Coca-Cola, bottled in Mexico, is still a gringo brand. The same holds true for Levi's, the quintessential American brand.

It doesn't matter where your brand is conceived, designed, or produced, its name and its connotations determine its geographic perception. Häagen-Dazs might have been developed in New Jersey, but its origins sound Scandinavian.

A number of years ago we met with the chairman of the SMH Group, the company that makes the Swatch watch. "What would you think about an automobile made in Switzerland?" he asked.

"Great," we replied. "We have the perfect advertising headline: Runs like a watch."

"I'm glad you like the concept," he said. "We're going to call the new product the Swatch car."

"Wait a minute," we added. "Swatch is an inexpensive fashion watch you wear a few times and throw in the dresser drawer. An automobile is a serious product and a serious investment. People define themselves by what they drive. If you want to give your new car a watch name, call it a Rolex."

But he didn't listen. The company used the Swatch name while the car was under development (first in a joint venture with Volkswagen and then later with Mercedes-Benz). Recently, wiser heads prevailed and the name was changed to the Smart car.

Smart thinking. The Smart car is now available in Europe as a fuel-efficient, low-pollution car for congested cities.

The choice of the Smart name for a global product illustrates a trend in global branding: the use of English words for brands that may have no connection with the United

The Mercedes-Benz Smart car was originally called the Swatch car when it was under development by the Swiss watch manufacturer. A Swatch car might be all right in Switzerland, but it's not a good name for a global brand.

Recently the Coca-Cola Company introduced KMX, a new energy drink to compete with Red Bull. Does KMX have a chance to carve out a significant share of the energy drink market? Of course not. It's way too late.

A French lemonade called Pschitt! is highly unlikely to be a big seller on the global market. Pschitt is a name that definitely does not work in English.

Kingdom, the United States, Canada, Australia, or any other English-speaking country.

Take a new energy drink invented in Austria. The amino acid–infused, caffeine-injected, detoxifying, carbonated drink was not called *"Roter Stier."* Instead, the manufacturer used the English words "Red Bull."

Red Bull has become an "in" drink in Europe and has also become a big brand here in the United States.

The top three high-end brands of blue jeans ($100 and up) all have English names, but none of them are American. Replay and Diesel are made in Italy. And Big Star is from France.

English has become the second language of the world. If you are going to develop a brand name for use on the world-wide market, the name better work in English. It doesn't have to be an English word, but it should sound like one.

In addition, care should be taken when translating English slogans into other languages. Sometimes the results can be disastrous. For example: "Come alive with the Pepsi generation," translated into Chinese, comes out as "Pepsi brings your ancestors back from the grave."

The Perdue slogan, "It takes a strong man to make a tender chicken," translated into Spanish means: "It takes an aroused man to make a chicken affectionate." And the Coors beer tag line, "Turn it loose," in Spanish becomes "Suffer from diarrhea."

While we encourage one global message for a brand, sometimes changes must be made to accommodate languages other than English.

19   THE LAW OF CONSISTENCY

A brand is not built overnight. Success is measured in decades, not years.

The most frequently violated law is the law of consistency.

A brand cannot get into the mind unless it stands for something. But once a brand occupies a position in the mind, the manufacturer often thinks of reasons to change.

"The market is changing," cries the manufacturer, "change the brand."

Markets may change, but brands shouldn't. Ever. They may be bent slightly or given a new slant, but their essential characteristics (once those characteristics are firmly planted in the mind) should never be changed.

If the market swings another way, you have a choice. Follow the fad and destroy the brand. Or hang in there and hope the merry-go-round comes your way again. In our experience, hanging in there is your best approach.

Tanqueray is the leading high-end gin. But Absolut and Stolichnaya have created a trend toward high-end vodkas. So Tanqueray introduces Tanqueray vodka.

Will Tanqueray vodka cut into the Absolut market? Of course not.

Will Tanqueray vodka undermine the Tanqueray gin market? Ultimately, yes.

Tanqueray should stick with gin and hope the market swings in its direction.

Tanqueray is a gin, so why would consumers buy Tanqueray vodka? If they wanted vodka, they would buy Absolut, Stolichnaya, or Smirnoff.

BMW has been the ultimate driving machine for twenty-five years. What's even more remarkable is the fact that BMW retained its strategy even though the brand was driven through three separate advertising agencies. A change of agencies usually signals the beginning of the end of a brand's consistency.

Jack Daniel's beer? Another silly idea that went nowhere.

Brands are used as personality statements. (Some marketing people call these statements "badges.") Your choice of a badge is often determined by the statement you want to make to friends, neighbors, coworkers, or relatives. Sometimes it is determined by the statement you want to make to yourself. "I drive a BMW."

As people grow up, they often want to change their personality statements. When kids grow up, they inevitably want to make a statement about their newfound maturity by changing brands . . . from Coca-Cola to Budweiser, for example. If Coca-Cola decided to try to retain these customers by "moving with the market," it would then logically introduce a product called Coca-Cola beer.

As foolish as Coca-Cola beer might seem to you, conceptually it's no different from Tanqueray vodka, Coors water, or Crystal Pepsi. Markets may change, but brands should stay the same.

In the liquor business, bourbon and whiskey are known as brown goods and gin and vodka as white goods. There may be a trend from brown to white (and there is), but should Brown-Forman introduce Jack Daniel's vodka? We think not.

Of course it did allow the introduction of Jack Daniel's beer and Jack Daniel's coolers. The beer went nowhere and was killed. The coolers continue to hang on, but what does a sissy cooler brand do to Jack Daniel's core image?

There may be a trend to Mexican food (and there is), but should a French restaurant add fajitas to its menu? We think not.

Brand building is boring work. What works best is absolute consistency over an extended period of time. Volvo has been selling safety for thirty-five years. BMW has been the ultimate driving machine for twenty-five years.

When people do boring work, they get bored. So every once in a while, someone at a company like Volvo gets a bright idea. "Why should we limit ourselves to dull, boring, safe sedans? Why don't we branch out into exciting sports cars?"

So Volvo recently launched a line of sports cars and even a convertible. What will a ragtop do for the Volvo brand? Nothing—except dilute its safety message.

Meanwhile, BMW introduces a station wagon version of the ultimate driving machine. "Hey, why limit ourselves to carefree yuppies? We need to have a vehicle for the young urban professionals when they grow up, get married, and have kids." (Have you ever driven a station wagon through the cones on a test track?)

How can Volvo, a company that built its reputation on safety, introduce a convertible? It doesn't make any sense.

What did the station wagon do for BMW? Nothing, except erode the driving image in the mind of the consumer.

Consistency built the Little Caesars brand, and lack of consistency is in the process of destroying the Little Caesars brand.

"Pizza! Pizza!" became the chain's rallying cry. Where else could you get two pizzas for the price of one? The power of this branding program made Little Caesars the second-largest pizza chain in America.

"Why should we limit ourselves to take-out pizza only?" the bored executives asked. So Little Caesars introduced "Delivery. Delivery." And promptly fell to third place in sales, after Pizza Hut and Domino's Pizza.

It gets worse. In order to turn the chain around, Little Caesars went big. The small pizza became a medium-size pizza. The medium-size pizza became a large pizza. And the large pizza became an extra-large pizza.

Talk about confusion. "I'd like to order a medium-size pizza, please."

"Do you want a Pizza Hut medium, which is actually our small size? Or do you want a Little Caesars medium, which is actually a Pizza Hut large?"

"Uh . . . do I still get two pizzas for the price of one?"

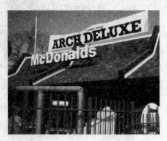

McDonald's heavily promoted a hamburger for adults called the "Arch Deluxe." But McDonald's is a place for kids, so naturally the Arch Deluxe was a failure.

"Pizza! Pizza!? No, we don't do that anymore."

A pity. Little Caesars had one of the best brands in the pizza category. The only brand focused on takeout. The only brand with an identity and a message. (Pizza! Pizza!) And now it has nothing. Another victim of the law of consistency.

Actually, many Little Caesars stores are drifting back to the two-for-one strategy that the company should never have abandoned in the first place.

McDonald's has been a kid-oriented family hamburger place for decades. "Why should we limit ourselves to kid-oriented products? Why not introduce an adult hamburger to compete with Burger King and Wendy's?"

So the Arch Deluxe was born. One hundred fifty million dollars' worth of advertising later, the Arch Deluxe is declared a disaster. And McDonald's quietly decides to drop it from the menu.

Notice one thing. It's always the product that is declared a failure, never the branding concept. McDonald's is a kid-oriented family restaurant. In such a setting, an adult hamburger might taste good in the mouth, but it is not going to taste good in the mind.

Run up a red flag whenever you hear the words: "Why should we limit ourselves?"

You should limit your brand. That's the essence of branding. Your brand has to stand for something both simple and narrow in the mind. This limitation is the essential part of the branding process.

Limitation combined with consistency (over decades, not years) is what builds a brand.

Rome wasn't built in a day. Neither is a brand of Romano cheese.

20   THE LAW OF CHANGE

Brands can be changed, but only infrequently
and only very carefully.

Having harped on the idea of consistency and focus, why
would we bring up the concept of change?

Because nothing in life, nothing in branding, is ever
absolute. There are always exceptions to every rule. And the
law of change is the biggest exception to the laws of branding.

Where does the change occur? Companies are often
focused on what they need to do internally in order to facili-
tate the change of a brand. The procedures, the manuals,
the brochures, the press conferences, the advertising, the
marketing.

But brand changing does not occur inside a company.
Brand changing occurs inside the mind of the consumer. If
you want to change your brand, keep your sights on your
target: the consumer's mind.

There are three situations where changing your brand is
feasible.

YOUR BRAND IS WEAK OR NONEXISTENT IN THE MIND

This is the easiest situation of all. In essence, there is no
brand, so you can do anything you want with the brand
name. Use it on a totally different product in a totally different category, if you will. Who's to know?

Citibank is in the process of
changing from a corporate
bank to a consumer bank. It
plans to make Citibank the
first global consumer bank.
It will take a while, but it can
be done. So far, so good.
But now comes the merger
with Travelers Group, which
threatens the entire
branding process.

The Intel 4004 was the world's first microprocessor, or computer on a chip. Subsequently Intel decided to get out of the D-RAM business and focus on microprocessors. A brilliant decision.

In 1985, Intel made a dramatic decision to get out of D-RAM (dynamic random access memory) chips in order to focus on microprocessors, a product Intel invented. In the process, Intel made its name the best-known worldwide brand of microprocessor. "Intel Inside" became the theme of a brand-building program of exceptional power. (In many cases customers are more concerned with the brand name of the processor than they are with the brand name of the personal computer.)

Intel changed its brand from D-RAMs to microprocessors. But except for a handful of computer executives and purchasing agents, who knew that Intel used to stand for D-RAMs?

YOU WANT TO MOVE YOUR BRAND DOWN THE FOOD CHAIN

If you are permanently lowering the price of your brand, you can often move it down the price ladder without hurting the brand. Customers will believe they are getting a lot of value by purchasing your brand. It's not necessarily a bad move. Marlboro lowered its cigarette prices and gained market share.

There's a lot of prestige in building Rolls-Royces, but not a lot of profit. Sometimes prices get out of line and permanent adjustments need to be made.

Going in the other direction, moving up the food chain, is much harder if not impossible. Holiday Inn Crowne Plaza was a difficult sell until the chain dropped the Holiday Inn from the name.

Marlboro once was a woman's cigarette, but few people knew that. So using cowboy imagery, Marlboro was able to change to a masculine cigarette.

YOUR BRAND IS IN A SLOW-MOVING FIELD AND THE CHANGE IS GOING TO TAKE PLACE OVER AN EXTENDED PERIOD OF TIME

Twenty-five years ago Citicorp (and its Citibank subsidiary) was about 80 percent corporate and 20 percent consumer. Today the numbers are almost reversed. Citicorp is about 30 percent corporate and 70 percent consumer.

Citicorp is successfully moving its Citibank brand from a corporate to a consumer perception. But the key concept to keep in mind is that little change has actually occurred in the mind of the banking prospect. Instead of "changing" minds, Citicorp has allowed enough time to pass so that the natural process of "forgetting" takes place.

What works in banking just won't work in a fast-moving field like computers or consumer electronics. There's not enough time for the "forgetting" process to take place.

Customers are never wrong. That's one of the many human traits that is so endearing and yet so frustrating from a branding point of view. When you try to tell customers that your brand is different than it used to be, they will reject your message.

• Xerox computers? No, Xerox is a copier.

• Gatorade energy bars? No, Gatorade is a sports drink.

• Epson computers? No, Epson is a computer printer.

In a famous Miller Lite television commercial, the beer drinker sees an ex–football player and says, "You're ah . . . you're ah . . . you're ah . . ."

"Nick Buoniconti," says the football player helpfully.

"No, that's not it."

Funny and also true. What you think your brand is really doesn't matter. It's only what your customer thinks your brand is that matters.

Kentucky Fried Chicken has been trying to walk away from the "fried" in its name for a long time. First, it changed the name of the chain to "KFC," but that didn't help much because customers say to themselves, "What do those initials stand for?" Second, it promoted its rotisserie chicken as the healthier alternative to fried chicken.

Guess what happened? People still went to KFC for fried chicken. Recently, KFC threw in the towel and went back to

Kentucky Fried Chicken is trying to walk away from "fried" chicken by changing its name to KFC. But consumers think to themselves, "What do those initials stand for?" And they end up with Kentucky Fried Chicken.

promoting fried chicken. "We're going to brag about the original recipe," said one franchisee, "the one that brought us to the dance."

You can be sure that the concept that brought your brand to the dance is still firmly embedded in your prospect's mind.

If you want to change your brand, first look into the prospect's mind. Where are you? Perhaps you're not in the mind at all. Fine, change away.

But if you are in the mind, and if you have a unique and distinct perception, then change your brand at your own risk. It's going to be a long, difficult, expensive, and perhaps impossible process.

Don't say we didn't warn you.

21   THE LAW OF MORTALITY

No brand will live forever. Euthanasia is often the best solution.

While the laws of branding are immutable, brands themselves are not. They are born, they grow up, they mature, and they eventually die.

It's sad. Companies are willing to spend millions to save an old brand, yet they resist spending pennies to create a new brand. Once you understand the nature of branding, you'll know when it is time to let your old brand die a natural death.

Opportunities for new brands are constantly being created by the invention of new categories. The rise of the personal computer created opportunities for Compaq, Dell, Intel, Microsoft, and many other brands.

But the rise of the personal computer also put pressure on established minicomputer brands like Digital, Data General, and Wang.

It's like life itself. A new generation appears on the scene and goes off in exciting new directions. Careers are born and blossom. Meanwhile, the old generation withers and dies.

Don't fight it. For brands, like people, there is a time to live and a time to die. There is a time to invest in a brand and there is a time to harvest a brand. And, ultimately, there is a time to put the brand to sleep.

"Tide's in. Dirt's out." The rise of detergent brands like

Film photography is slowly being replaced by digital photography. But Kodak refuses to face that reality. Instead it is trying to save the brand by using the Kodak name on its digital products.

Procter & Gamble's Tide put pressure on laundry soap brands like Rinso, which eventually faded away.

Companies make serious errors of judgment when they fight what should be a natural process. Yet the Nursing Home for Dying Brands does a booming business with millions in advertising and promotional dollars being spent to keep terminally ill brands on life-support systems.

Don't waste money on walkers and wheelchairs. Spend your money on the next generation. Invest your money in a new brand with a future.

Many managers make poor financial decisions because they fail to distinguish between two aspects of a brand's value.

- How well known the brand is

- What the brand stands for

A well-known brand that doesn't stand for anything (or stands for something that is obsolete) has no value. A brand that stands for something has value even if the brand is not particularly well known.

You can do something with a brand that stands for something. When you stand for something, you at least have the opportunity to create a powerful brand. This is especially true in the area of publicity.

What's a Kraft? Who knows? When a brand is just well known but doesn't stand for anything, it doesn't lend itself to publicity and other branding techniques. It has nowhere to go but down.

What's a Kodak? A conventional camera and conventional photographic film. But that market is slowly shifting to digital photography.

Look what happened to the 8mm motion picture camera and film. For amateurs at least, film cameras are dead. They have been almost totally replaced by electronic systems using videotape. So how did Kodak try to compensate for the loss of the amateur movie film business it used to dominate? Of course. It put its Kodak brand name on videotape cassettes.

Does the Kodak brand dominate the videotape business? Of course not. Kodak stands for photography. The Kodak brand has no power beyond the realm of conventional photography.

But videotape is only a side skirmish to the main battle that is developing between photographic cameras and digital cameras. Long term, Kodak's billion-dollar photographic business is in jeopardy. Will the market go digital?

History is not on Kodak's side. The slide rule has been replaced by the pocket calculator. The analog computer has been replaced by the digital computer. The record album has been replaced by the compact disc. Analog cellular phones are being replaced by digital phones.

In music, television, and telephones, the trend has been to digital. The average automobile today has more digital computing power than an IBM mainframe had not too many years ago.

Fight or flee? As you might have expected, Kodak has decided to do both. And, in our opinion, Kodak is making major branding mistakes on both sides of the street.

Take the photography side of the street. Kodak has been the major driver in the creation of the Advanced Photo System. Based on a new 24mm film and new electronic control systems, APS gives you a choice of three print formats, plus a lot of other advantages. Besides Kodak's massive up-front investment in APS, the scheme requires photo shops to spend hundreds of millions of dollars for new film-processing equipment.

(You know that Kodak spent a lot of money on developing the APS system, because it even gave it a new name, the Kodak Advantix system.)

The question is obvious. Why spend all that money on conventional photography if the market is going digital?

Kodak tried to use its name on videotape, with very little success. Kodak stands for photography, not videotape.

Kodak has launched a major attempt to move its brand name into digital photography. Will this work? Probably not. What Kodak needs is a second brand that stands for "digital."

Wouldn't it be better to let the old system die a natural death and use the money to build a new digital brand?

Meanwhile, on the digital side of the street, Kodak is also making a serious error (and this might be its biggest mistake of all). Instead of launching a new brand, Kodak is venturing into the field with the Kodak brand name (Kodak Digital Science).

It will never work. In the first place, there are too many competitors in the market with a digital reputation that Kodak lacks. To name a few: Canon, Minolta, Sharp, Sony, and Casio. Even more important, when a revolutionary new category develops, the inevitable winner is a revolutionary new brand name.

When miniature electronic products became technically feasible, the winning brand was not General Electric, RCA, or Zenith. It was Sony, a brand-new brand.

When videotape rentals of motion pictures became commercially feasible, the winning retail brand was not Sears, 7-Eleven, or any supermarket or drugstore chain. It was Blockbuster Video, a brand-new brand.

When personal computers invaded the office field, the winning brand was not IBM, AT&T, ITT, Hewlett-Packard, Texas Instruments, Digital, Unisys, Motorola, Sony, Hitachi, NEC, Canon, or Sharp. It was Dell, a brand-new brand.

Whatever happened to Rinso White and Rinso Blue? Almost none of the soap brands survived the detergent era. Will the photography brands do any better in the digital era?

It remains to be seen, but our best guess is no.

22   THE LAW OF SINGULARITY

The most important aspect of a brand is its single-mindedness.

- What's a Chevrolet? A large, small, cheap, expensive car or truck.

- What's a Miller? A regular, light, draft, cheap, expensive beer.

- What's a Panasonic? At one point in time, Panasonic was a computer, computer printer, facsimile machine, scanner, telephone, television set, and copier, among other things.

These are all burned-out brands because they have lost their singularity. They could, of course, remain on the marketing scene for many years because of the line-extension generosity of their competitors. But make no mistake about it. Loss of singularity weakens a brand.

What's an Atari? An Atari used to be a video game, the leading video game as a matter of fact. Then Atari tried to become a computer.

What's an Atari? A brand that has lost its life because it lost its singularity.

It's this singularity that helps a brand perform its most important function in society.

What's a brand? A proper noun that can be used in place of a common word.

Volvo has been selling safety for some thirty-five years. In the process, the brand has become one of the largest-selling European luxury cars in the United States. In a recent decade, Volvo sold 849,348 cars in America, ahead of BMW (804,968) and Mercedes-Benz (770,089).

Even though Wal-Mart sells everything, the brand is not an exception to the Law of Singularity. Wal-Mart owns the "low price" position in the mind.

- Instead of an imported beer, you can ask for a Heineken.

- Instead of an expensive Swiss watch, you can ask for a Rolex.

- Instead of a thick spaghetti sauce, you can ask for Prego.

- Instead of a safe car, you can ask for a Volvo.

- Instead of a driving machine, you can ask for a BMW.

What's a brand? A singular idea or concept that you own inside the mind of the prospect.

It's as simple and as difficult as that.

THE

11

IMMUTABLE
LAWS OF
INTERNET
BRANDING

1   THE LAW OF EITHER/OR

The Internet can be a business or a medium, but not both.

Putting your brand name on a Website doesn't make it an Internet brand. There are brands and there are Internet brands, and the two are quite different.

If you want to build an Internet brand, you shouldn't treat the Internet as a medium, you should treat it as a business.

But the Internet is a medium, you might be thinking, just like newspapers, magazines, radio, and television. Maybe so, but if you want to build a powerful Internet brand, you will have to treat the Internet as an opportunity, not as a medium. You will have to treat the Internet as a totally new business where the slate is wiped clean and where endless opportunities await those who can be first to create new categories in the mind.

- It wasn't ABC, NBC, CNN, the *New York Times*, the *Wall Street Journal*, *Time* magazine, *Business Week*, or *Newsweek* that created the most successful information site on the Internet. It was Yahoo!

- It wasn't Barnes & Noble, Waldenbooks, or Borders that created the most successful bookseller on the Internet. It was Amazon.com.

It wasn't any of the big media companies that created the most successful information site on the Net. It was David Filo and Jerry Yang, two grad school dropouts.

Internet
Internet
Television
Radio
Magazine
Newspaper

No new medium has ever replaced an existing medium. A new medium changes existing media, but it does not replace them.

- It wasn't Sotheby's or Christie's that created the most successful auction site on the Internet. It was eBay.

- It wasn't AT&T, Microsoft, or Cablevision that built the most successful provider of Internet service. It was America Online.

Everyone knows the Internet will change their business as well as everybody else's business. But how? And what can you do about it? It's easy to err in one of two different ways. You can make either too much of the Internet or too little.

You make too much of the Net when you assume that it will completely replace traditional ways of doing business. No new medium has ever done that. Television didn't replace radio. Radio didn't replace magazines. And magazines didn't replace newspapers.

You make too little of the Net when you assume it will not affect your business at all. Every new medium has had some effect on every business, as it has had on existing media. Radio, for example, was primarily an entertainment medium until the arrival of television. Today radio is primarily a music, news, and talk medium.

Great, you might be thinking. We'll play the Internet right down the middle. We'll treat it as another arrow in our marketing quiver. That would be your biggest mistake of all. You fracture your brand when you try to make it an Internet brand as well as a physical or real-world brand. No brand can be all things to all people. Yet that is what many Internet experts recommend.

To quote one Internet guru: "Internet commerce needs to be part of a broader electronic business strategy, a strategy that embraces all the ways that you let your customers do business with you electronically: by touch-tone phone, by fax, by e-mail, by kiosk, via handhelds, and via the Web."

Many brand owners follow this strategy. They carry their

existing brands over to the Internet and wait for miracles to happen. So we have sites like the following:

- Levi.com, Dockers.com, Barbie.com

- ABC.com, Forbes.com, Washingtonpost.com

- Ford.com, GM.com, Daimlerchrysler.com

Does brand familiarity in the "outernet" foster interest in the Internet? A study by Forrester Research among sixteen- to twenty-two-year-olds says "no." According to the Cambridge, Massachusetts–based firm, "Some of the hottest brands in the off-line world have no online value."

That's not surprising. Did any nationally recognized newspaper or magazine make the transition to television? No, they were all failures on the tube, most notably *USA Today* and *Good Housekeeping*. (*USA Today on TV* lost an estimated $15 million the first year and was canceled during its second season.)

Business managers have much in common with military generals who fight their next war with the previous war's weapons. Witness the wave of Websites that mimic the real world.

Slate magazine, introduced by Microsoft with a blaze of publicity, is a typical example. Edited by a semicelebrity (Michael Kinsley, made famous by CNN's *Crossfire*), *Slate* struggled along as a Web version of a conventional magazine, including a conventional subscription price of $29.95 a year.

Only twenty-eight thousand people subscribed. So *Slate* switched to a more typical Web subscription price, zero dollars a year. Traffic to the *Slate* site zoomed to 2.4 million visitors a month. The question is, how will Microsoft make money by giving away the magazine?

The obvious answer is with advertising, which we don't think will work either. *Salon*, another magazine-type periodical,

Very few media brands have managed to make the transition from one medium to another. *USA Today on TV* was a noteworthy failure.

www.ries.com

We have a Website that uses our name, but it's a site set up for information only. No business takes place at www.ries.com.

has been published on the Web ever since 1995. In spite of the fact that it has been attracting 2.5 million visitors a month, the publication is still unprofitable. Last year it posted revenues of just $3.5 million, mainly from advertising.

As a matter of fact, the magazine is not a good analogy for the Internet. Nor for that matter are radio, television, books, or newspapers. The Internet is the Internet, a unique new medium with its own unique new needs and requirements. Building a brand on the Internet cannot be done by using traditional brand-building strategies.

On the Internet, you should start the brand-building process by forgetting everything you have learned in the past and asking yourself these two questions:

1. What works on the Internet?

2. What doesn't work on the Internet?

Hopefully these laws will provide the answers you need to build a powerful Internet brand. The material is not based on strategies that have worked in other media. Rather, it is based on our experience with developing strategies for dozens of Internet start-ups. What worked and what didn't work.

Which leads to the first and most crucial decision you must make: For my product or service, is the Internet going to be a business or a medium?

If the Internet is going to be a business, then you must start from scratch. You must develop a totally new strategy, a totally new way of doing business, and (most important of all) a totally new name.

Who is going to win the Internet book war, Amazon.com, Barnesandnoble.com, or Borders.com? Is there any question in your mind that Amazon.com will be the big winner? There shouldn't be. If the Internet is a business, putting your name on both your physical store and your Website is a serious error.

If any company should have an advantage in selling books on the Web, it's Barnes & Noble. They are the largest bookstore chain in America and the best-known bookstore brand. Yet their Internet brand has not been very successful.

Who is going to win the Internet bank war, Citibank.com, Chase.com, or BankofAmerica.com?

None of the above. The bank war will be won by one of the Internet-only banks. (Unless, of course, none of the Internet-only banks do a good job of branding.) Why? Banking is going to be a business on the Internet, not a medium.

If the Internet is going to be a medium, then you can use your existing brand name. The Internet becomes a complement to or replacement for existing media, be they radio, television, direct mail, newspapers, or magazines.

In truth, the Internet is a good information medium, an electronic library, if you will. Every company that has a sizable business needs a Website to keep its customers and prospects informed about the range of products and services it offers, as well as prices, delivery dates, warranties, colors, sizes, customer testimonials, and so on.

Instead of asking the customer to shuffle through out-of-date catalogs or spec sheets, a well-designed Website can present up-to-date information in a hierarchical and interactive way. (For the first time, a paperless office is within the realm of possibility.)

The Web should simplify many ordinary business transactions. If you want to subscribe to *Newsweek*, once you are connected to your service provider you should be able to type *www.newsweek.com* into your browser, go to the *Newsweek* site, and subscribe. Inputting your name, address, and credit card or bank account number should do it. No cards falling out of the magazine, no stamps, no trips to the post office, no phone calls.

In this example you'll notice that the product doesn't change. *Newsweek* is still a magazine delivered weekly by the U.S. Postal Service. The Internet is a medium that simplifies the selling of the product. It might also allow you to sample the product so you can decide whether or not you want to subscribe.

**Amazon.com
vs.
Barnes & Noble**

Currently Amazon.com sells six times as many books as Barnesandnoble.com (since shortened to bn.com). Furthermore, Amazon's book business is profitable, while Barnes & Noble's Website is losing buckets of money.

Dell Computer is a textbook example of a company that is moving its business from one distribution channel (the telephone) to another (the Internet). Ultimately Dell should consider dropping phone sales (a higher-cost distribution method) and taking all orders online.

For some brands, of course, the Internet will replace existing distribution methods. (Any business that relies heavily on the telephone is a good candidate for moving to the Web. Flowers and pizza delivery are two obvious candidates.)

Three big brands that rely heavily on the phone (Dell, Cisco, and Charles Schwab) are moving to the Internet using their same names.

Dell Computer is in the process of shifting to selling on the Internet. It won't happen overnight, of course, but you can visualize the day when most of Dell's business will be done on the Net. (Currently the Internet accounts for about 50 percent of the company's revenues.)

For Dell the Internet has paid off in more ways than just increased revenues. It has helped the company cut sales and administrative costs from 15 percent of revenues five years ago to an estimated 9 percent currently.

Cisco Systems, the world's largest supplier of network equipment, has also moved to the Net. Today Cisco conducts more than 75 percent of its business over the Internet. The move to the Internet has reduced the lead time needed to fill orders from three weeks to three days. While total revenue has grown 500 percent, the number of employees required to service requests has grown by only 1 percent.

Charles Schwab is also shifting from the phone to the Net. It has become the leading online broker with more than three million Internet accounts (and thousands more added daily). Today Schwab handles about 236,000 trades a day, 80 percent of which are placed electronically.

Initially, Charles Schwab thought it needed a separate name for its Internet operation, so it came up with the "eSchwab" name. Recently the company shortened the name to *www.Schwab.com*.

The Schwab situation illustrates two important principles. One, the same name can be used as long as your business will be moving to the Net. Two, on the Internet, the shorter the name the better. Charles Schwab is not a partic-

ularly long name, but the company decided to shorten it to
"Schwab" on the Web.

If you have a choice, don't take a chance on a long name.
When prospects have to type a name on a keyboard, they are
going to gravitate to the shorter names.

Merrill Lynch is also making a move to the Internet; presumably using both its existing name (*www.MerrillLynch.com*)
and its initials (*www.ml.com*). That is a mistake. Unlike Charles
Schwab, Merrill Lynch is not going all the way. Its Internet
move is only a half step. The firm obviously has no intention of
giving up the 14,800 well-paid stockbrokers who generate most
of its business.

The Merrill Lynch Website could function as an information source for the customers who do business with its
brokers. But not as a separate business. If Merrill Lynch
wants to use the Internet as a business, the firm needs to
come up with a separate name.

With 30 to 35 percent of all stock trades by individuals
already on the Internet, Merrill Lynch is in a different position than Schwab. It only has four choices:

1. Do nothing. Not a bad idea. There will always be people
   who want the personal attention of a financial consult-
   ant. Furthermore, by doing nothing Merrill Lynch can
   portray the negative side of Internet trading. It's hard to
   badmouth the Charles Schwab competition when you
   are offering the same services as they are.

2. Make the same move that Charles Schwab did and shift
   the business to the Internet. It's probably too late in the
   game for this to work. Furthermore, what does the firm
   do with its fourteen thousand brokers and its reputation
   for service?

3. Set up an Internet brokerage business with a separate
   name. This is what Merrill Lynch should have done . . .
   years ago.

Merrill Lynch is not bullish
on the Internet. In the long
run their failure to develop
an Internet brand will hurt
them. But in the short run,
with the market going
sideways, customers are
making fewer trades on
their own and returning to
full-service stockbrokers.

4. Use the Merrill Lynch name on both businesses, which is what they are doing. This is a "foot-in-both-camps" strategy that will never work. In the long run it will undermine the reputation of Merrill Lynch. It was not long ago that Merrill's brokerage chief, John Steffens, publicly stated that "the do-it-yourself model of investing, centered on Internet trading, should be regarded as a serious threat to Americans' financial lives."

Trust is an important ingredient in any retail business. If your customers don't trust you, they are unlikely to continue to do business with you. You undermine that trust by speaking out of both sides of your mouth. A company should take a stand and stick with it. That's the way to build rapport with customers over a long period of time. Sometimes it's more important to be consistent than to be "right."

In any industry, there's room for multiple approaches, but there may not be room for multiple approaches in the same company under one brand. For many smaller companies, the best strategy might be to move lock, stock, and barrel to the Web.

Hoover's, Inc. started out as a bookstore and then a publisher of business books. Its first book, *Hoover's Handbook 1991: Profiles of Over 500 Major Corporations*, was an enormous success. The company went on to publish a number of other business and reference books.

Today, however, Hoover's, Inc. is primarily an Internet company selling corporate profiles and other reference material to a wide range of companies and institutions. Eighty-four percent of the company's revenues now come from its Web services.

Provident American was a small Hartford insurance company that decided to jump on the Net. So it sold off its traditional underwriting business and severed its relationships with some twenty thousand agents. Then it changed its name to HealthAxis.com and became an Internet company

Publishers of directories are going to encounter shrinking markets for their products unless they move their businesses to the Web, as Hoover's has successfully done.

selling health insurance from a variety of major carriers at prices 15 percent lower than it had been selling off-line. Recently HealthAxis metamorphosed into an ASP selling insurance technology software on-line.

Larry Latham was an auctioneer specializing in selling repossessed single-family homes from hotel ballrooms across the country. In spite of booming sales of $600 million a year, he decided to shut down his company's fourteen branch offices and move to the Internet. He hired a staff of twenty-two computer experts and renamed the company "Homebid.com." In a test of the site he sold 136 out of 147 homes over the Web at prices that averaged 97 percent of list.

Larger companies are big enough to have the resources to support both an Internet business and an off-line business. In general, however, they need to differentiate between the two by giving their Internet business a different name.

Amway, the world's largest direct-sales company with $3 billion in annual sales, decided to take its unique distribution system to the Internet. But not with the Amway name. Its new Internet name is Quixtar.com.

Procter & Gamble is using the Web to sell beauty products, but not with Oil of Olay or any of its other brand names. Instead, P&G has created a new name (Reflect.com) and a new strategy. The site will allow consumers to "personalize" their selection of beauty products.

How can you tell whether the Internet is a business or a medium for your brand? You need to ask yourself the following questions:

1. **Is the brand tangible or intangible?** For tangible products the Internet tends to be an information medium. For intangible products, a business. Intangible products that are particularly appropriate for Internet branding include banking, insurance, stock brokerage, and the like.

We expect financial services of all types to move to

So far Quixtar has done quite well. It's now the leading Website for health and beauty products. There's even a book on the subject, *The Quixtar Revolution* by Coy Barefoot.

Boo.com

Fashion products are not going to do well on the Web. In spite of $135 million in investment capital and reams of favorable publicity, Boo.com went belly-up. When it comes to doing business on the Net, forget fashions and think basics.

the Net. The savings can be substantial. American Express estimates that it saves $1.00 every time a card-holder checks a balance on the Web rather than over the phone.

Travel is another category that is moving to the Web. In the year 2001, travelers spent $14 billion buying tickets on the Internet, amounting to 14 percent of their total airline spending.

2. **Is the brand fashionable or not?** For fashionable products the Internet tends to be a medium. For other products, a business. Clothing is generally fashionable, while computers are generally not. Where fashion is the primary factor, it's difficult to imagine much business going to the Web.

We don't predict much success for Nordstrom-shoes.com, even though the site was launched with a $17 million advertising campaign. The commercials are amusing, but the prospect is unlikely to do much shoe buying on the Internet. There are three major questions a shoe site can't answer. Will they fit? Will they look good on my feet? Are they going to be comfortable?

3. **Is the product available in thousands of variations?** If so, the Internet tends to be a business. Books, for example. It's hard for an existing retail establishment to compete in a category with a bewildering array of choices. There's no way, for example, that a bookstore could stock all the titles available at Amazon.com.

Another category that seems likely to move to the Web is office supplies. Again, the choices are so overwhelming that no one physical store can carry everything a company might want to buy.

Product variation is likely to become a major battleground in an Internet-dominated economy. Excluding food stores, roughly half the people who shop at any given store today walk out without buying anything. The major reason: The store didn't have in stock the product the customer was looking for.

Now that customers have the ability to find anything they want on the Web, manufacturers need to respond in one of two ways.

If physical stores are your major distribution channel, then you need to reduce the product variety you offer. Compaq's best response to Dell, for example, would have been to reduce its product line and promote a handful of computer products available off the shelf in retail computer stores. When you make too many variations, you can be sure that the one model the prospect wants won't be in stock.

If the Internet is your major distribution channel, then you want to promote the wide range of models, sizes, and colors you have available.

4. **Is low price a significant factor in the brand's purchase?** If so, the Internet tends to be a business—eBay.com and Priceline.com, for example.

The ability of the buyer to quickly check prices on a large number of sites is making the Internet a very price-sensitive medium. There are even sites, like MySimon.com and DealTime.com, that will compare prices among other sites by sending out robots, or "bots," to check the prices. Heaven help you if you don't have a competitive price.

Because of this price pressure, one of the biggest challenges for building a brand on the Net is trying to figure out how to make money. This will be a critical issue for many brands.

Automobiles are another category where the Internet is likely to change buying patterns. Carpoint.msn.com, Autobytel.com, and other car-buying sites are beginning to establish themselves as brands. The reason is simple: It's easy to make price comparisons on the Net. And there isn't any haggling with a salesperson.

A typical Staples retail store carries 8,000 items, but their Website offers some 200,000 items.

Three retail revolutions:
1. Branding.
2. Self-Service.
3. The Internet.

The Internet is the third revolution in retailing. The first (branding) eliminated the sales pitch needed to sell a product. The second (self-service) eliminated the salesperson. The third (the Internet) will eliminate the middleman in the distribution channel. Each revolution reduced the cost of selling.

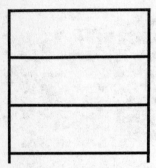

We recently tried to buy bookcases on the Internet, but the cost of delivery would have been as much as the cost of the bookcases, so we said no thanks.

5. **Are shipping costs a significant factor as compared to the purchase price?** If so, the Internet tends to be a medium. Groceries, for example. Webvan has already failed and Peapod.com is struggling. It's unlikely that any mass-market Internet site will be able to build a successful business and a successful brand selling groceries.

The milkman used to deliver fresh milk every morning. We're sure that many families would like their milk delivered today, but they can't get it. Why? It's not economical anymore.

The grocery clerk used to go in the back and get your selections off the shelves, but not anymore. Self-service is a lot more economical.

In the Internet era, are we going to go backward? Is self-service dead? We don't think so. Yet many marketing experts are saying the opposite. "The grocery store as we know it is going out of business," said former Procter & Gamble brand manager Doug Hall.

Futurist Faith Popcorn goes even further. By the year 2010, she predicts, 90 percent of all consumer products will be home-delivered. "They'll put a refrigerator in your garage and bar code your kitchen. Every week they'll restock your favorites, without your ever having to reorder. They'll even pick up your dry cleaning, return your videotapes, whatever you need."

The Internet is the biggest technological development of the twentieth century, but let's not get carried away. Just because something is possible doesn't make it likely to occur. The grocery business has three strikes against it: (1) high selection costs, that is, the costs involved in picking and packing products in the warehouse; (2) high delivery costs; and (3) low margins. The average supermarket chain makes 1 or 2 percent net profit on sales.

It's hard to see how an Internet company could absorb the additional costs involved in picking, packing, and delivery and still make money in a low-margin business. A niche market, to be sure, but not a mainstream brand.

Hope springs eternal. Venture capitalists doled out an astounding $275 million to launch Webvan, an Internet grocery company. In addition, the company managed to hire as its chief executive George Shaheen, the former head of Andersen Consulting (now Accenture).

The total investment in Webvan reached almost $1 billion before the online grocer was shut down on July 9, 2001.

Some consultants claim that you need both an Internet presence and a retail presence to be successful in the future, the so-called click and mortar strategy. Otherwise, goes the argument, how could you return items you ordered on the Net? That's one reason some experts have foolishly predicted that Barnesandnoble.com will eventually outsell Amazon.com.

Don't believe it. People don't buy things based on how easy they are to return. It's a factor, of course, but not the primary factor in deciding where to buy. Reputation, selection, and price are far more important. It's impossible to build a reputation as a store with great selection and low prices if you are schizophrenic, that is, if you have both physical stores and Internet sites. All you are doing is confusing people.

Will Sears.com become a big success? Unlikely.

No one factor, of course, will determine whether your brand should be a business on the Internet or whether the Net is just another medium to promote your brand. You have to carefully consider all the factors before you decide.

But decide you should before some other brand beats you to the punch.

2   THE LAW OF INTERACTIVITY

Without it, your Website and your
brand will go nowhere.

Not since television took off in the early fifties has the nation seen such a technological revolution as the Internet. For a time, Internet usage was literally doubling every month.

There is a relationship between television and the Internet. Each is a communications medium. And nothing on earth affects more people in a more powerful way than the introduction of a major new mass-communications medium.

Over the course of human history, there have been five such introductions:

1. The book

2. The newspaper, or periodical, which includes magazines

3. Radio

4. Television

5. The Internet

(While the telephone is a communication device and has had a long-lasting effect on people's lives, it does not possess the characteristics of a mass-communications medium.)

Life gets complicated. The new medium does not replace the old. Rather, the new medium is layered on top of the old media, forever changing and modifying all of the existing media.

- The original mass-communications medium, of course, was the human voice, still an unusually effective way to send a message. Each major medium to follow became powerful in its own right because the medium possessed a unique and highly prized attribute.

- The book **multiplied** the number of people that could be reached by a single individual. Not only could millions of people share ideas and concepts, but these ideas could also easily flow from one generation to the next.

- The periodical added the attribute of **news**. Large numbers of people could share news of the latest events in their city or country and eventually the world. In essence, the periodical took the printing process used in book production and greatly sped it up. Where a book could take months to produce (and still does, unfortunately), a newspaper could be produced overnight.

- Radio added the attribute of the **human voice**. News and entertainment could be communicated with emotion and personality. A long line of celebrities have used the emotional power of radio to communicate in an exceptionally effective way—Winston Churchill, Franklin D. Roosevelt, Rush Limbaugh, Dr. Laura Schlessinger, and Howard Stern, to name a few.

- Television added the attribute of **motion**. Radio, with moving pictures, if you will. Motion pictures, of course, were the precursor of television and still represent much of TV's content. Movies were, and still are, a powerful, emotional medium, but not a mass-communications

A new medium creates changes that go well beyond the medium itself. Before television the most popular sport in America was baseball. Today the most popular sport is football. Why? Most people watch sports at home on their television sets, and football produces better moving pictures than baseball.

medium. You have to go to a theater to see a film when it is first released.

• And the Internet? What attribute does the Internet bring to the communications table?

If the Internet is going to take its place alongside the other major media, it will be because it exploits a totally new attribute.

We believe that history will rank the Internet as the greatest of all media. And the reason is simple. The Internet is the only mass-communications medium that allows **interactivity**. (The organization that was formed to promote Internet advertising is called, appropriately enough, the Interactive Advertising Bureau.)

On the Internet a brand lives or dies in an interactive environment. In the long run, interactivity will define what works on the Internet and what doesn't work. The secret to branding on the Internet is your ability to present your brand in such a way that your customers and prospects can interact with your message. You'll have to throw out many of the traditional ways of brand building.

Take advertising, for example. Will traditional advertising be effective on the Internet? Of course not.

Face the facts. People generally dislike advertising. Why do people love the TV remote control or zapper? It allows quick channel surfing when ads appear.

With the Internet, your prospects have total control of what they see, read, and hear. Is there any reason to doubt that they won't turn off your advertising message as soon as it starts?

Along with advertising, many of the traditional forms of communication are just not going to make it on the Net. Take newspapers and magazines as another example. Why would you assume that you could publish a successful magazine or newspaper on the Internet? Where is the interactivity?

About the only "interactivity" a newspaper or magazine format allows on the Net is the ability to read stories in any order you choose. But you can do that now with a paper publication. (Many newspaper readers start with the sports section. And *Playboy* "readers" have been known to start with the centerfold.)

Putting a print magazine on radio or television never worked either. Literally dozens of publications tried to take their successful print periodicals into the radio and television arena. They all failed. Why? The essence of radio is the human voice and the essence of television is motion. A printed piece just sits there; it says nothing and doesn't move.

Slate isn't the only Internet magazine that is slowly slipping out of sight. *Salon* magazine was voted the best Website of 1996 by *Time* magazine, yet the on-line publication continues to lose money: $40 million since its founding in 1995. "The future of media is on-line," argues *Salon* publisher Michael O'Donnell. We beg to differ. Print is print; the Internet is the Internet. Trying to combine the two is a serious strategic error.

TheStreet.com is a newspaper format trying to make it on the Internet. In spite of a raft of publicity generated by its cofounder James Cramer, the site continues to generate nothing but red ink. In the year 2000, TheStreet.com had $23.3 million in revenues (mostly from advertising) and managed to lose $69.1 million.

Advertising is drying up on the Internet as more and more companies recognize the futility of advertising in an interactive medium. Where do Internet sites spend most of their own advertising dollars? Surprisingly, it is not on the Net but in the traditional media of television, newspapers, and radio.

One successful publication on the Web is the Interactive Edition of the *Wall Street Journal*, which currently has almost 600,000 paying readers. One reason for its relative success, of course, is the price. The Interactive Edition of

Slate.com

Slate is one of dozens of publications that have tried to make it on the Net. In spite of the deep pockets of its owner, Microsoft, Slate has consistently lost money. You can't take a format that works in one medium (magazines) and transfer it to another medium (the Internet).

The Wall Street Journal newspaper couldn't get *The Wall Street Journal Magazine* off the ground. It is extremely difficult, if not impossible, to take a brand from one medium and transfer it to another.

the *Journal* is a big bargain. While the regular paper subscription goes for $175 a year, the Interactive Edition is just $59 a year and only $29 a year if you are already a print subscriber.

We wonder whether or not Dow Jones would have been better off launching an Internet publication under a different name and with greater interactivity.

Perhaps the most successful Internet publication is *Consumer Reports Online,* with 590,000 subscribers. That makes sense because "interactivity" is an important aspect of how a subscriber might use the on-line publication. If you want to buy a refrigerator, you can key in "refrigerator" and find out what brands the nonprofit organization recommends. Yet the on-line publication has been a mixed blessing for *Consumer Reports.* In two years, the number of subscribers to the print publication has dropped from 4.5 million to 4 million.

In this connection, look at the success of *60 Minutes*, a television show that was number one in the Nielsen ratings for a number of years. Although *60 Minutes* has a magazine-like look, it was created especially for television using a personality-driven format. Furthermore, *60 Minutes* did not lock itself into an existing magazine name.

What works in one medium won't necessarily work in another. As a matter of fact, chances are great that one medium's success will be another medium's failure.

- What newspaper also became a successful magazine brand? None that we know of. (The *Wall Street Journal* tinkered with a publication called the *Wall Street Journal Magazine*, but the publication went nowhere.) The only successful newspaper "magazines" are the ones published on Sunday and given away free with the papers. Not exactly our idea of successful brands.
- What successful television brand also became a successful cable television brand? None that we know of.

The big cable television brands—HBO, ESPN, CNN, A&E, MTV, QVC, Showtime, and Nickelodeon—were not line extensions of broadcast brands. They were new brands created especially for cable.

Yet too many companies lock themselves into the past. They look for ways to use yesterday's name on tomorrow's medium. News Corp., for example, the owner of *TV Guide* magazine, is using the *TV Guide* name on a cable channel as well as an Internet brand called TV Guide Online. Neither strategy is going to work very well.

If you want to build a brand on the Internet, you need to build a new brand designed specifically for the new medium. In other words, you have to build interactivity into your site, and you generally need a new name.

It bears repeating. The difference between the Internet and every other medium is interactivity. Unless your site has this crucial ingredient, it is going to get lost in cyberspace.

The competition is intense. There are already many more dotcom Websites than there are registered trademarks filed in the United States.

Interactivity is not just the ability to select from a menu. (You can do that with a book or a magazine by looking at the index. You can also do that with a phone by pressing numbers. You can do that in a restaurant by asking for the wine list.)

Interactivity is the ability to type in your instructions and have the site deliver the information you requested in the form you requested it. Check out Amazon.com. Type in a subject and the site will present a list of books that match your category. You can do the same with authors or a title.

(Instead of asking for the wine list, try asking the sommelier for a list of all French red wines that cost less than $40 a bottle. There's no interactivity in a restaurant menu and no sense of humor in a sommelier.)

Interactivity is also the ability of the site to furnish additional information based on your original query. Select a book to purchase at Amazon.com and the site will give you

| Domains: 28.2 million |
| Trademarks: 2,468,611 |

There are 28.2 million .com, .net, and .org registrations on the Internet as compared with only 2.5 million U.S. trademark registrations. The proliferation of Internet brands makes the branding process very difficult.

One of the phenomenal successes on the Internet has been the auction site eBay. It's a site that takes full advantage of the interactive capabilities of the Net. Furthermore, like almost all enormously successful Internet sites, eBay is a unique business with no real-world analogies.

the names of at least three other books bought by previous buyers of the book you ordered.

Interactivity is also the ability to add your own information to the site. The best Internet sites are two-way streets. At Amazon.com you can rate books by giving them anywhere from one to five stars, and in addition you can submit short reviews, which are posted within hours under the book you reviewed.

Interactivity is also the ability of a site to handle complex pricing situations almost instantaneously. Take airline tickets, for example. An airline site is able to select from a multitude of fares, flights, dates, and conditions and give you a price on the spot, which you can either accept or decline. They can even recommend a flight schedule that offers the lowest priced fare. (The Cisco site is another Internet operation that makes good use of this on-the-spot pricing technology.)

Interactivity is also the ability of the site to perform a wide variety of tests: intelligence tests, driving tests, occupational aptitude tests, psychological tests. Some of these areas are going to turn into big brands and big businesses.

Interactivity is also the ability of the site to conduct auctions of all types. Priceline.com and eBay are two big brands that have already taken advantage of this capability. (Currently eBay is worth $12 billion on the stock market. And Priceline.com is worth $672 million.)

Interactivity is also the ability of the site to diagnose a situation and suggest remedies. We worked with a famous personality to develop a personal Website. The first screen was going to be a menu of various problems that an individual might be experiencing.

"Don't do it that way," we suggested. "Make the screen interactive. Ask the person a series of questions, then let your computer tell the individual what his or her problem might be."

Interactivity is a powerful metaphor for the patient-doctor or the student-teacher relationship.

You visit a medical doctor and describe your symptoms. The doctor diagnoses your problem and prescribes appropriate treatment. This is the kind of interactivity that is possible on the Internet.

Will the Internet spawn successful medical and educational brands? Why, of course. These are disciplines based on interactivity.

CapellaUniversity.com, for example, offers five hundred courses in forty areas of specialization, including an MBA program with extensive instruction in e-business operation and management. You can be sure there will be many more Capellas to come.

Contrast correspondence courses by mail with Internet educational ventures. The best that current correspondence courses can accomplish is a weekly or semiweekly dose of interactivity. The Internet can greatly speed up the process.

3   THE LAW OF THE COMMON NAME

The kiss of death for an Internet brand is a common name.

The importance of the name was the key concept in *Positioning*, now available in a twentieth-anniversary hardcover edition.

The most important marketing decision you can make is what to name the product.

So we said in *Positioning: The Battle for Your Mind*, a book published in 1981. So how does the Internet change the role of the brand name?

In the positioning age, the name was important. In the Internet age, the name is critical.

There's a reason for that. In pre-Internet days, a brand always had a visual component. While the name was the most important element, the visual also influenced the brand's purchase. The shape of a Coca-Cola bottle, the colors on a box of Kodak film, the typography of an Intel logotype, the look and location of a McDonald's restaurant.

The Internet wipes out the visual. To tap into a Website, you type in a word. No pictures, no colors, no typography, no look, no location.

If the name is critical, then why are most brand names on the Web so bad? That's putting it mildly. Most Internet brand names are not bad: They're terrible.

Some typical Internet brands include Advertising.com, Buy.com, Communities.com, Cooking.com, Cruise.com, Desktop.com, eToys.com, Flower.com, Garden.com, Gear.com, Gifts.com, Hardware.com, Hifi.com, HomePage.com,

Images.com, Individual.com, iMotors.com, Ingredients.com, Law.com, Mail.com, Mortgage.com, Office.com, Pets.com, Phone.com, Postcard.com, Sales.com, Songs.com, Sports.com, Tickets.com, Vote.com, Weather.com, Wine.com, Women.com.

None of these are small, insignificant companies. Major corporations or venture capitalists have heavily funded them all. Many also tapped into the stock market. To cite four examples: Pets.com raised $50 million in an initial public offering, Mortgage.com raised $60 million, iMotors raised $137 million, and eToys raised $166 million. All four dotcoms are now bankrupt or have shut down operations.

What's wrong with these brand names? They're all common, or generic, names.

A common noun is a word that designates any one of a class of beings or things. *Cars* is a common noun.

A proper noun is a word that designates a particular being or thing. *Mercedes-Benz* is a proper noun.

Traditionally, brand names have been proper nouns. (If you were a language purist or work for the U.S. Trademark Department, you would call brand names "proper adjectives," as in "Mercedes-Benz cars." But most people use brand names as nouns. They will say, "I drive a Mercedes," not "I drive a Mercedes car.")

The best-known, most valuable brand names in the world are all proper nouns, not common or generic names. There are seventy-five worldwide brands worth more than $1 billion each, according to Interbrand, a brand consulting group. And none of these are common or generic names.

Typical brands on the top seventy-five list include Coca-Cola, Microsoft, Ford, Disney, Intel, McDonald's, Marlboro, Nokia, Nescafé, Hewlett-Packard, Gillette, Kodak, and Sony. (Together, the seventy-five brands, according to Interbrand, are worth an incredible $912.1 billion.)

A few years from now are you likely to find Cola.com, Software.com, Cars.com, Kids.com, Chips.com, Hamburgers.com, Cigarettes.com, Cellphones.com, Coffee.com, Com-

The customer owns the brand.

You own your trademark, your manufacturing facilities, and your distribution channels, but you don't own your brand. The customer owns the brand. The value of a brand resides in the perception of the brand inside the prospect's mind.

Enjoy Coca-Cola

The world's most valuable brand is Coca-Cola. According to Interbrand, the brand is worth $72.5 billion, an astounding 65 percent of the company's market capitalization.

Books.com is owned by Barnes & Noble, as is Book.com. We bet that many more prospects use the brand name barnesandnoble.com or bn.com to connect to the site than use the common or generic names.

puters.com, Razors.com, Photos.com, or Electronics.com on the list of the world's most valuable names? We think not.

"But the Internet is different" is the cry you hear from thirty-year-old CEOs managing Internet start-ups. You don't have to wear suits, you don't have to wear ties, you don't have to wear shoes, you don't have to make money, you get stock options worth millions, and you can use generic names for your Websites.

But is it? Is the Internet really different when it comes to brand names? So far it doesn't seem to be.

- The leading Internet service provider is not ISP.com. It's AOL.

- The leading search engine on the Net is not Searchengine.com. It's Yahoo!

- The leading retailer of books on the Net is not Books.com. It's Amazon.com.

- The leading job-search site on the Net is not Jobs.com. It's Monster.com.

- The leading auction site on the Net is not Auction.com. It's eBay.

- The leading airline-ticket bid site on the Net is not Airlineticketbid.com. It's Priceline.com.

- The leading travel site on the Net is not Travel.com. It's Expedia.com.

- The leading electronic greeting card is not Greeting-Card.com. It's Bluemountain.com.

As it happens, there are two Internet names on Interbrand's list of the seventy-five most valuable brands. AOL, worth $4.5 billion, and Yahoo!, worth $4.4 billion. You'll notice that both AOL and Yahoo! are proper nouns, not common nouns.

In spite of all the evidence to the contrary, why do most

Internet executives continue to prefer using common names rather than proper names for their Websites? There are three reasons.

1. When the Internet was new, when there were few sites up and running, when few people knew the names of any Websites, a common name was an advantage. You wanted to look for a site selling shoes, you typed in "shoes.com."

    It was like an old-fashioned grocery store. You wanted crackers, you asked for the crackers. You wanted oatmeal cookies, you asked for the oatmeal cookies. Today, however, there are many brands of cookies and many brands of crackers in a supermarket. You don't ask for crackers, you ask for Ritz crackers. You don't ask for oatmeal cookies, you ask for Pepperidge Farm oatmeal cookies.

2. When the Internet was new, many companies jumped on the Internet with common names. After all, a common name was the fastest, most direct way to communicate what the site was all about. The common name also made it easier for users to navigate the Net.

    The advantages of a common name lasted for about two weeks as thousands and then hundreds of thousands of Internet sites were set up. Today, with more than five million dotcoms in operation, the advantages of a common name for an Internet site are nil.

3. Now that the Net has been around for a few years, Internet companies are having trouble getting beyond the mind-set of those early days. They still think a common name is the best approach. In some ways, this is a self-reinforcing situation. As everyone launches common name sites, every newcomer thinks this must be the way to go. And so that's the way they go.

    With his *Candid Camera*, Allen Funt exploited human nature to do what others are doing regardless of whether or not it makes sense. His favorite episode involves an elevator where the first person goes into the car and faces the front. The next three people, all *Candid Camera* confederates, get into the elevator and face the rear. By the time the fifth person comes in, the first one feels so uncomfortable that he turns around and also faces the rear.

Face the facts. Just because most sites use common names doesn't mean that a common name is the best strategy for your site. It only means that most Internet operators are under group pressure to conform.

One of the reasons for the dotcom disaster is the almost universal use of common-name Websites. Some samples of this common-noun craziness are as follows:

- In automobiles: AutoConnect.com, Autosite.com, Auto-Trader.com, Autoweb.com, Cars.com, CarsDirect.com, and CarOrder.com.

- In banking: Ebank.com, Telebank.com, and Netbank.com.

- In diamonds: eDiamonds.com, InternetDiamonds.com, and WorldDiamonds.com.

- In employment: ComputerJobs.com, Gotajob.com, Headhunter.net, and Jobs.com.

- In facsimile: eFax.com, Fax.com, and Jfax.com.

- In finance: 401k.com, eCoverage.com, eCredit.com, Loansdirect.com, eHealthinsurance.com, eLoan.com, Loanwise.com, Mortgage.com, and Studentloan.com.

- In furniture: BeHome.com, Decoratewithstyle.com, Ezshop.com, Furniture.com, FurnitureFind.com, Furnitureonline.com, Housenet.com, and Living.com.

- In groceries: Food.com, NetGrocer.com, and HomeGrocer.com.

- In health and nutrition: eDiets.com, eNutrition.com, HealthQuick.com, and onHealth.com.

- In pets: Petco.com, Pets.com, and Petstore.com.

- In postage: E-Stamp.com, Stamps.com, and Simple-postage.com.

- In prescription drugs: Drugstore.com, YourPharmacy.com, and Rx.com.

- In real estate: Cyberhomes.com, eProperty.com, Goodhome.com, Homeadvisor.com, Homebid.com, Homegain.com, Homes.com, Homeseekers.com, Home-store.com, Myhome.com, Ourhouse.com, Owners.com, RealEstate.com, and Realtor.com.

- In shopping: IStopShop.com, Buy.com, BuyItNow.com, Netmarket.com, NowOnSpecial.com, ShopNow.com, and Shopping.com.

- In travel: Cheaptickets.com, Lowestfare.com, TravelHoliday.com, and Trip.com.

Millions of dollars' worth of advertising turned the Sock Puppet into the Internet's first icon. Yet how many people connected the puppet with Pets.com or were motivated to buy something from the site? Lack of profits led Pets.com to be put to sleep for good.

These are not generic names picked at random from the millions of dotcoms on the Internet. Many of these dotcoms are no longer with us, of course, but all of them were serious sites backed by serious venture capitalists and supported by millions of dollars' worth of advertising.

- Art.com was spending $18 million a year on advertising.

- AutoConnect.com was spending $15 million a year on advertising.

- CarsDirect was spending $30 million a year on advertising.

- Drugstore.com was spending $30 million a year on advertising.

- Homestore.com was spending $20 million a year on advertising.

- Living.com was spending $20 million a year on advertising.

- Pets.com was spending $20 million a year on advertising.

- Petstore.com was spending $10 million a year on advertising.

- RealEstate.com was spending $13 million a year on advertising.

- Rx.com was spending $13 million a year on advertising.

These CommonName.coms were just a small sample of the thousands of Internet companies trying to spend their way into the prospect's mind. For the most part it was money down the rat hole. There's no way that even a small percentage of these common-name sites could make it.

(It's a sign of the times that one of the most heavily hyped advertising agencies specializing in the Internet field calls itself Agency.com.)

Will some of these generic names be successful? Sure. In the land of the blind, the one-eyed man is king. Nobody is going to stop drinking beer because all of the beer brands use generic names. Nobody is going to stop buying on the Web just because all the Internet brands are generic.

In the absence of competition, people will buy from a site with a common name. But as sites are set up with strong "proper" brand names, the common-name sites are going to dry up and blow away.

You have to win in the mind. And the mind treats common or generic names as representative of all the sites in the category. Not just a single site.

In the human mind all automotive sites are "car dotcoms." How could Cars.com ever establish a singular identity separate from the other car dotcoms?

In the mind all furniture sites are "furniture dotcoms." How could Furniture.com ever establish a singular identity separate from the rest of the furniture dotcoms?

The vast majority of brand names on the Web are purely

generic names. Most of these sites are now bankrupt or out of business.

What's an eToys? An e-toy is a toy purchased on the Internet. An eToys is a company that sells e-toys on the Internet.

The name eToys is a weak brand name, yet the stock market thinks differently. On the first day that eToys went public, the stock price nearly quadrupled in value, making the company worth $7.7 billion, 35 percent greater than that of its retail rival, Toys "R" Us Inc. (In its last fiscal year eToys lost $73 million on revenues of $34.7 million.)

One of the problems with a common name like eToys is the ability of competition to jump in the marketplace and claim similar names.

- eToy.com

- iToy.com

- iToys.com

- Toy.com

- Toys.com

- Toystore.com

- iToystore.com

- eToystore.com

Not unexpectedly, eToys filed for bankruptcy and shut down its site on March 7, 2001.

Naturally eToys tried to register these and other similar names. But where do you stop? And how much will it cost? And will the legal system allow one company to own all the sites with "toy" in the name?

What's an E*Trade? An e-trade is a stock purchase or sale made on the Internet. An E*Trade is a company that handles e-trades on the Internet.

A generic name like E*Trade is weak. The mind thinks

In spite of its expansion into electronic banking and the opening of a $12 million retail center in Manhattan, we forecast hard times ahead for an Internet brokerage firm with a common name like E*Trade. It's almost impossible to build a brand with a common name.

verbally, not visually. E-trade is the name of the category, not the company. Furthermore, you can't use an asterisk in the actual site name. In order to reach E*Trade, you have to type in www.etrade.com.

Even though E*Trade has the enormous advantage of being first on the Internet, the company has already fallen to second place in terms of customer-trading volume online. (Charles Schwab is the leader.)

Massive advertising in the mass media is keeping E*Trade in the game. But with stock trading down, E*Trade has been losing money. In a recent year, the company lost $242 million on revenues of $1.3 billion. How long it can continue to expand its services while at the same time losing money is a question that only the future can answer.

How can we be so sure that proper names will prevail over common names as brand names on the Internet? The only proof we can offer you is a hundred years of history. In the past century, how many common names have become successful brands?

Very, very few.

Few categories in the outernet, as opposed to the Internet, are dominated by generic brand names. Invariably they are dominated by proper or "name" names.

- In automobiles, we have Ford, Chevrolet, Chrysler, Volvo, and Mercedes-Benz.

- In banking, we have Citibank, Chase Manhattan, and Wells Fargo.

- In drugstores, we have CVS, Eckerd, Rite-Aid, Walgreen's, and Osco.

- In furniture, we have Ikea, Ethan Allen, Levitz, Roche-Bobois, and Maurice Villency.

- In groceries, we have Kroger, Safeway, Winn-Dixie, Publix, and Pathmark.

- In department stores we have Macy's, Saks Fifth Avenue, Marshall Field, Nordstrom, and Neiman-Marcus.

- In discount stores we have Wal-Mart, Kmart, and Target.

But the Internet is different, you might be thinking. There must be a reason for the rash of generic names.

The Internet is different, but the mind of the prospect stays the same. To be successful you have to position your brand name in the mind.

What managers often forget is that the mind treats a generic or common word as the name for a category of things, not as one particular thing or brand.

No automobile dealer would call his or her dealership "Cars." Why not? Imagine the following conversation.

"Where did you buy your new car?"

"At Cars®."

"Huh. What did you say? I asked you what dealership you bought your new car from."

With literally thousands of Websites using generic names, you can expect the same type of dialog to occur.

"What discount broker do you use on the Internet?"

"Mydiscountbroker."

"I know, but what's his name?"

"Mydiscountbroker."

"I already asked you that."

This is not a laughing matter. It demonstrates the way the mind works. Words get put into categories. A common name gets put into a different category than a proper name.

The comedy team of Abbott and Costello based their classic baseball routine on the confusion that can occur when one class of words is substituted for another.

"Let's see, we have on the bags, Who's on first. What's on second. I Don't Know is on third."

"That's what I want to find out. Who's on first?"

"Yes."

Mydiscountbroker

Even the Website's television commercials make fun of the Mydiscountbroker name. When your advertising agency admits that your name is a problem, maybe your name is a problem.

The Better Mousetrap never became a popular brand of mousetrap even though it might have been a better mousetrap.

"I mean, the fellow's name?"

"Who."

"The first baseman?"

"Who."

"The guy playing first?"

"Who is on first."

"I'm asking *you*, who's on first?"

"That's the man's name."

"That's who's name?"

"Yes."

Many companies in the past hundred years have tried to use common-type nouns as brand names in their categories. Just check the trademark register. There's a host of brand names that have tried to preempt a category by using a common-sounding name. Some examples:

- Toast'em toaster pastries

- Soft & Dri deodorant

- Soft 'N Gentle toilet tissue

- Soft Shave shaving cream

- Nice 'N Soft facial tissues

- NA nonalcoholic beer

- Baby's Choice disposable diapers

- Kid Care adhesive bandages

Tell the truth. Do any of these generic brand names ring a bell with you? Probably not. It's hard to remember a brand that uses a common name.

One of the best examples of the futility of trying to build a brand with a common name is Lite, the first light beer. When Miller Brewing introduced Lite beer, there was no

"Miller" on the can. And no competitor could use the word "Lite" on a beer brand either because Miller owned the trademark.

Miller launched Lite with a massive advertising program and the segment took off. As you might have expected, many competitors jumped in with generic versions of their own. Schlitz Light, Coors Light, Bud Light.

Even though Miller was first with Lite beer, even though Lite had the benefit of tremendous amounts of advertising and publicity, Miller was forced to throw in the towel and rename the product Miller Lite.

You can see the problem. The beer drinker goes into the bar and says, "Give me a Lite beer." And the bartender says, "Fine. What kind of light beer do you want?"

Some categories, of course, are loaded with mostly generic brand names. (Group pressure at work.) What is interesting is that in these categories, generally no one brand will dominate the category. Breakfast cereals are a good example—brands like Corn Flakes, Bran Flakes, Frosted Flakes, and 100% Granola.

Take the "bran" category. There are dozens of "bran" brands trying to capture the category. Some examples:

- Kellogg's All-Bran

- Kellogg's Bran Flakes

- Kellogg's 40+ Bran Flakes

- Kellogg's Raisin Bran

- Nabisco 100% Bran

- Post Bran Flakes

- Post Raisin Bran

- Total Raisin Bran

Lite had the enormous advantage of being the first light beer in the mind, yet the generic name turned out to be a serious disadvantage. Renamed Miller Lite, the brand currently is a poor second to Bud Light and will probably lose out to Coors Light, too.

One of the few cereal brands with a proper name instead of a common one, Cheerios is also the leading brand of breakfast cereal.

AllBooks4Less.com

An Internet bookstore focused on selling books for less than Amazon.com might have a chance to be successful, but not with a common name like AllBooks4Less.com.

As a result of the overwhelming reliance on common names, the cereal category has no clear-cut brand leader. The largest-selling cereal brand has a market share of about 6 percent. (Cheerios is one of the few cereal brands that doesn't use a common name.)

If common names don't work on the outernet, why should they work on the Internet? The problem is exactly the same. How do I get the prospect to remember my brand name and associate it with some positive attribute?

When you use a common name as a brand name, you have little chance to do either. First, the prospect can't differentiate between your site name and the category name. Second, you can't associate a specific attribute with the name because the name stands for the entire category, not just your site.

Some sites try to solve this problem by combining the attribute with the common noun. Instead of Books.com, the brand name becomes AllBooks4Less.com. Or perhaps Cheaptickets.com or Lowestfare.com.

Ironically, this is a branding strategy that can have a modicum of success in the outernet but not on the Internet. If you're driving down the road and see a sign that says "All Books 4 Less," you know what the store is selling and why you might want to shop there. (A chain named "All Books 4 Less," on the other hand, is still not going to outsell Barnes & Noble, Waldenbooks, or Borders.)

On the Internet you don't drive down the road and you don't see the AllBooks4Less sign. You are going to have to remember the name and that's not going to be easy.

You ask your mind, "Who sells all books for less on the Net?" And the answer comes back "Amazon.com."

In the short term, however, many prospects are using search engines to find sites that might interest them. So a name like AllBooks4Less.com could conceivably attract a fair number of hits. But that's only in the short term.

The whole idea of branding, on the Internet or elsewhere, is to burn your name in the mind. When you can successfully do that, there's no need for the prospect to use a search engine to find your Website. So in the long run, your Internet brand name will have to stand on its own. And a common name is a very weak foundation to stand on.

"Cars" is not a good name for an automotive dealership. And Cars.com is not a good name for a Website that sells cars. Neither is Mydiscountbroker.com a good name for a stockbroker on the Internet.

And what do you suppose Internet.com is all about? This is a brand that has two strikes against it. Internet.com is a common noun used for a Website that tries to appeal to everybody for everything. (You can hear the shouts of joy in the corridors at Internet.com. "Wow! We were able to register the best name on the Net." Don't be too sure.)

What's your own name? Brown, Jones, Smith? Would you consider changing your name to a generic? If you did, a phone conversation might sound like this:

"Hello, this is Some Person."

"I know that, but what's your name?"

In spite of our arguments to the contrary, there will be intense pressure inside most organizations to take the common-name route. It's the lemming effect. Once the crowd takes off in one direction, everyone just naturally joins in and follows. There's some psychological satisfaction in following the crowd. In art, in music, in clothing, and in Internet brand names.

"It is better for your reputation to fail conventionally," John Maynard Keynes once said, "than it is to succeed unconventionally."

Don't say we didn't warn you.

Even worse than a common name is trying to create a brand by using a symbol. In spite of his attempt to use this symbol as a name, the rock musician was invariably called "the artist formerly known as Prince." Recently he gave up on the symbol and went back to being a Prince.

4 THE LAW OF THE PROPER NAME

Your name stands alone on the Internet,
so you'd better have a good one.

The torrent of generic brand names on the Internet provides hope for the late starters. If you can launch a Website with a good idea and a good brand name, you are in a good long-term position. You can wait until the generic site names drop out of sight and then jump in and win big.

Make no mistake about it. Your name stands alone on the Internet and is by far your most valuable asset. This is one of the major differences between the Internet and the physical world.

In the physical world, there are many clues to a company's purpose. Location, window displays, even the size and architecture of the building. A hotel looks like a hotel, a bank looks like a bank, and a restaurant looks like a restaurant.

Even in the industrial field, you seldom are exposed to just the company's name. A brochure or direct-mail piece will usually have pictures that establish the company's product line or service.

On the Internet, however, the name stands alone. Until you get to the site, you won't find any clues to what the site actually does.

In the physical world, a mediocre name can sometimes work because the physical clues combine to establish the company's identity. A watch store looks like a watch store.

The location and visual look of a retail store, for example, can be so unique that customers often forget the store's name. "It's the repair shop at the corner of Eighty-seventh Street and York Avenue."

Even a droll name can work in a retail environment. "The Mattress Firm" for a bedding shop, for example. "The Money Store" for a home-loan company. "General Nutrition Centers" for a health-supplement store. Names like these never stand alone. They always carry a wealth of clues that communicate their real purpose.

In the electronic world, there are no clues. There are no books in the window that tell you that Amazon.com is a bookstore. No travel posters that tell you that Priceline.com sells airline tickets. No greeting cards that tell you what Bluemountain.com does.

This is what leads Internet companies astray. Straight into the generic trap.

The lure of the generic is so powerful that some companies have paid enormous sums for names that in the long run will turn out to be useless. A Los Angeles company bought Business.com for $7.5 million. (To whom it may concern: If you had bought this book for $18.95, you would have saved yourself $7,499,981.05). Some other recent purchases:

In the real world, generic names can work because the customer can refer to the brand by its physical location. "The dry cleaners at the shopping center," for example.

- Wine.com was bought for $3 million.

- Telephone.com was bought for $1.75 million.

- Bingo.com was bought for $1.1 million.

- Wallstreet.com was bought for $1.03 million.

- Drugs.com was bought for $823,456.

- University.com was bought for $530,000.

It's worse than tulip mania in Holland or truffle madness in France. The latest bid on the Loans.com name was $3 million. (If you own a common Internet name, our advice is to sell it before the mania melts away.)

Even at this early stage, the power of a proper name as opposed to a common name for an Internet brand has been clearly demonstrated. The big early winners (AOL, Amazon.com, eBay, Priceline.com, Yahoo!) have all been proper names rather than common names.

There's a lot of confusion on this issue. People see a name like Priceline and assume it's a common or generic name, but it's not. The generic name for the category is "tickets" or really "name-your-own-price airline tickets." Tickets.com is a common name used for a Website that, in our opinion, is not going to take off.

("Price" and "line" are common words, of course, but they are used out of context and in combination to create the proper name "Priceline," which becomes an effective Internet brand name.)

Every common name can also be a proper name if used to identify a single person, place, or thing. Bird is a common name, but it's also a proper name, as in Larry Bird or Tweety Bird.

When you are choosing a brand name for your Website, the first thing to ask yourself is, what's the generic name for the category? Then that's the one name you don't want to use for your site.

Invariably a singular proper name will turn out to be a better name for your site than a generic.

iVillage.com, for example, is a better name for a Website devoted to women than Women.com. (Yes, there is a Website called Women.com, and it spent millions to promote its name before selling out to a rival.

Ashton.com is a better name for a Website that sells luxury goods than Cyberluxury.com, eLuxury.com, or First-jewelry.com.

In the physical world, the same branding principles apply. The proper name is superior to the common or generic name.

iVillage.com vs. Women.com

It looks as if iVillage.com will emerge as the leading Website for women. It recently agreed to acquire its chief rival, Women.com, for about $30 million in stock and cash.

- McDonald's is a better name than Burger King.

- Hertz is a better name than National Car Rental. (All the car rental names you see in an airline terminal are national car rental companies, but there's only one Hertz.)

- *Time* is a better name than *Newsweek* or *U.S. News & World Report*.

- Kraft is a better name than General Foods, so when Kraft General Foods decided to simplify their name, they called the company Kraft and not General Foods.

There are degrees of commonness, of course. "Burger King" is not a totally common name. The Hamburger Place would be a totally common name for a fast-food establishment that features burgers.

There are degrees of properness, too. McDonald's and Hertz are more "proper" than *Time* magazine. *Time* is a common name used out of context to create a proper name.

In the same way, Amazon and Yahoo! are more "proper" than Priceline and eBay, which are common words used out of context. (All distinctions are relative, of course. Even Amazon and Yahoo! can be common words. A yahoo is a brutish creature and an amazon is a tall, vigorous, strong-willed woman.)

So how "proper" should your Website name be?

It all depends. First, and most important of all, you want your Website name to be perceived as a proper name. Then hopefully you want your name to be more "proper" than your competitors'. But you also want to consider other factors.

1. THE NAME SHOULD BE SHORT.

In general, the shorter the better. Shortness is an attribute even more important for an Internet brand than an outernet brand.

You have to keyboard the Website name into your computer. That's why the site name should be both short and easy to spell.

Hormel took the generic category "spiced ham" and shortened it to Spam, creating one of the world's better-known brands. Recently Hormel has been upset by the use of its brand name as the term describing junk e-mail.

Many Internet brands have two strikes against them. They are both too generic and too long. As a result, they are hard to remember and hard to spell. Some examples:

- Artsourceonline.com.

- Dotcomdirectory.com

- eBusinessisbusiness.com

- Expressautoparts.com

- Interactivebrokers.com

- GiftCertificates.com

- OnlineOfficeSupplies.com

- Treasurechestonline.com

Starting with the generic name for the category and condensing it is a good way to kill two birds with one stone. You create a proper name that's also short and easy to spell. CNET.com, for example, took the generic term "computer network" and shortened it to CNET, creating a short, proper name that's also easy to spell.

Sandoz needed a brand name for its over-the-counter flu therapy product. So the company reversed the word order and condensed the name to TheraFlu. The product went on to become the leading brand in its category.

Nabisco needed a brand name for its vanilla wafers, so it called them Nilla. And the powerful brand name Jell-O is just a shortened version of gelatin dessert.

Nabisco itself is a brand name constructed by condensing its former generic name, National Biscuit Company. (There are many national biscuit companies, but only one Nabisco.)

Barnesandnoble.com finally threw in the towel on their long, difficult-to-spell name and shortened it to bn.com.

Nilla became a brand name by dropping the first syllable of the generic category, vanilla wafers.

Morgan Stanley Dean Witter is an enormously success-ful financial company, but Morganstanleydeanwitter.com is not going to make it on the Internet. The company short-ened the name to msdw.com.

(The names bn.com and msdw.com are not good either, because they are hard to remember.)

The well-known consulting firm Booz Allen & Hamilton obviously couldn't use its long, complicated name on the Internet, so the firm launched Bah.com. (Not a particularly euphonious choice.) And what about names like Deloitte & Touche? Or PricewaterhouseCoopers?

The Internet will force many companies to take another look at their names. This is true even for companies for which the Internet is a medium and not a business. Instead of launching Bah.com, perhaps Booz Allen & Hamilton should have changed the consulting firm's name to Booz Allen and launched a site called BoozAllen.com.

And what about names like: Allegheny, Allegheny Tele-dyne, Allegiance, Anheuser-Busch, Bausch & Lomb, Canandaigua Brands, Di Giorgio, Harnischfeger, Hayes Lemmerz, Heilig-Meyers, Leucadia National, Marsh & McClennan, Phillips-Van Heusen, Rohm & Haas, Schering-Plough, Smurfit-Stone, Sodexho Marriott Services, Synovus Financial, Tecumseh Products, TIAA-CREF, Transmon-taigne, Wachovia, Wackenhut, Weyerhauser.

All of these companies will have difficulty transferring their names to the Internet. And these are not small compa-nies either. They are all ranked in *Fortune* magazine's list of the one thousand largest American companies.

Because of the Internet, many companies will have to sim-plify their names. You have to misspell a name and address pretty badly before the Postal Service will refuse to deliver your letter. To reach a Website, however, you have to be per-fect. You can't drop one of the periods or leave out a hyphen.

One way to have your cake and eat it too is by using

Good grief, what a lousy brand name, TIAA-CREF. There are thousands of names like TIAA-CREF's in the world that will never become powerful brand names.

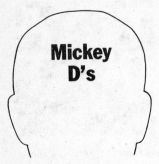

Among the hip crowd, McDonald's is commonly referred to as "Mickey D's." Should McDonald's change its name to Mickey D's? Of course not. Then the hip crowd would be forced to create a new nickname. "Anybody for MD's?"

both a name and a nickname on the Web. Charles Schwab is the leading discount brokerage firm, but on the Web the company uses both CharlesSchwab.com and Schwab.com, although it promotes only Schwab.com.

Ask Jeeves is one of the leading search-engine sites on the Internet, but it wisely operates with two site names: AskJeeves.com and Ask.com.

When you have to choose between several brand names that seem equally good, the smartest name to pick is usually the one that also has a good nickname.

People feel closer to a brand when they are able to use the brand's nickname instead of its full name.

- Beemer, not BMW

- Chevy, not Chevrolet

- Coke, not Coca-Cola

- Bud, not Budweiser

- FedEx, not Federal Express

- Mac, not Macintosh

2. THE NAME SHOULD BE SIMPLE.

Federal Express fell in love with its nickname and changed its name to FedEx. There's a certain dignity and maturity in the Federal Express name that is lost in the nickname. Keep your current name and let your customers use your nickname. You'll both be better off.

Simple is not the same as short. Simplicity has to do with the alphabetical construction of the brand name. A simple word uses only a few letters of the alphabet and arranges them in combinations that repeat themselves.

Schwab is a short name (six letters), but it is not a simple name because it uses six letters of the alphabet. This is one reason that Schwab is not a particularly easy name to spell.

Mississippi is a long name (eleven letters), but it is also a simple name because it uses only four letters of the alphabet. Which is why most people can spell Mississippi.

Coca-Cola is both a short name and simple name. Although the name has eight letters, it is formed by using only four letters of the alphabet. Furthermore, the name repeats the "co" syllable.

Pepsi-Cola, on the other hand, is a much more complicated name than Coca-Cola. Pepsi-Cola uses eight letters of the alphabet to form a nine-letter word.

Autobytel.com, for example, suffers from the same problem. Like the Pepsi-Cola name, it takes eight letters of the alphabet to form the name. Furthermore, how do you "parse" the name? Is it Auto by Tel or Auto Bytel? And what is a Bytel anyway?

Even though the Autobytel Website has a proper name, along with an early lead in the car category, we don't believe it will become the premier site in its category.

Some people have criticized Nissan's decision to change its U.S. brand from Datsun to Nissan. But from a brand-name point of view, Nissan is the superior name. Although both brand names use six letters, the Datsun name requires six letters of the alphabet and the Nissan name only four. (You hardly hear anyone use the Datsun name anymore.)

3. THE NAME SHOULD SUGGEST THE CATEGORY.

Here's the paradox. To become a big brand on the Web, you need a proper name. On the other hand, the name should suggest the category without falling into the generic name trap.

This is not an easy line to walk. Shortening the generic name is one way to achieve both objectives (CNET, Nilla, and Jell-O, for example).

Another approach is to add an "off-the-wall" word to the name of the category. PlanetRx, for example. (We would have preferred a different word than *planet*, which has been overused. In addition to the ailing Planet Hollywood chain, there are two other would-be planet brands on the Internet: Pet Planet and Planet Outdoors.)

Movie hits are commonly called "blockbusters," a term the company borrowed to create the memorable Blockbuster brand name for its chain of video-rental stores.

Branders.com has become the leading Website in the promotional products field.

DrugDepot.com might also have been a better name for an Internet drugstore than either Drugs.com or Drugstore.com. It's alliterative and mimics both the Home Depot and the Office Depot brands in the physical world.

We helped a company that was planning to sell advertising specialties on the Web come up with the name Brand-Builders.com. (The company sells hats, T-shirts, pens, binders, and other material used in corporate brand-building projects.) Then we agreed with the client to make the name more finger friendly by shortening it to Branders.com.

4. THE NAME SHOULD BE UNIQUE.

Unique is the key characteristic that makes a name memorable. This is true for all brand names, especially those used on the Web. AskJeeves.com and DrKoop.com are two Internet brand names that are both unique and memorable.

No name, of course, is totally unique unless you create it from scratch, like Acura, Lexus, Kodak, or Xerox.

AskJeeves.com is associated with the butler and DrKoop.com with the former surgeon general of the United States. But these are singular individuals who are not going to be confused with the Websites that carry their names.

As a matter of fact, both individuals suggest the functions of their sites—Ask Jeeves for finding information and Dr. Koop for medical information.

But how unique is More.com, a site that spent $20 million to tell you they sell health, beauty, and wellness products? Or MyWay.com or CheckOut.com or Individual.com or Owners.com or YouDecide.com or Indulge.com or This.com or Respond.com? Or any of a hundred different sites being backed by millions of dollars' worth of venture capital and promoted with millions of dollars' worth of advertising?

A Waltham, Massachusetts, company spent $20 million in television and radio advertisements to launch a gift-

More was apparently less. The Website lasted less than fifteen months before it was sold to HealthCentral.com for $6 million.

buying service called Send.com. How is anyone going to remember the name?

Let's say you wanted to buy a present for your friend Charlie for Christmas. Do you go to Buy.com, Present.com, Gift.com, or what?

By definition a common or generic name is not unique. It does not refer to a specific person, place, or thing like a proper name does. Therefore, a common name used as a Website name for the generic category is not memorable.

5. THE NAME SHOULD BE ALLITERATIVE.

Why do you think children move their lips when they read? They are converting the visual symbols represented by the letters and words into sounds that can be processed by their brains. The mind works with the sounds of words, not with the visuals and their shapes.

When you grow up, you learn not to move your lips when you're reading. But this doesn't change the way your mind works. It still works with the sounds of words.

If you want people to remember something, rhyme it for them. "If the glove don't fit, you must acquit."

Fogdog.com is an improvement over the brand's original name, which was Sportsite.com.

Alliteration is another sure-fire way to improve your brand's memorability. Many real-world brand names are alliterative. Some examples:

- Bed, Bath & Beyond

- Blockbuster

- Big Bertha

- Coca-Cola

- Dirt Devil

Send.com

Another generic Website that is likely to go nowhere in spite of a multimillion-dollar advertising program is Send.com.

Memorability is greatly enhanced when your brand name is alliterative like Dunkin' Donuts or Rolls-Royce.

- Volvo

- Weight Watchers

In our search of active, well-promoted Internet brands, we could find very few that used alliteration. (One of the reasons we liked BrandBuilders as a name was its alliteration.)

The same principle applies with babies. Give your newborn kid a head start. Pick a first name that's alliterative with your last name. It's a fact that many famous celebrities have alliterative names: Alan Alda, Ronald Reagan, Robert Redford, Tina Turner, Marilyn Monroe, Charlie Chaplin, Sharon Stone, Greta Garbo, Doris Day, Sylvester Stallone, Susan Sarandon, Ted Turner, Mickey Mouse, Donald Duck.

6. THE NAME SHOULD BE SPEAKABLE.

When was the last time you bought something because you read an advertisement or a news item about it? Many people are hard put to remember a single item they bought because of an ad.

Does this mean that advertising is ineffective? Not necessarily. Most people buy products or services because they hear about these things from friends, neighbors, or relatives.

Word of mouth is the most effective medium in your entire communications arsenal. But how does the first mouth get the word to pass along? From publicity or advertising, of course.

As a rule of thumb, there are ten word-of-mouth recommendations for every publicity or advertising "hit." This ten-to-one ratio holds for many different products and services.

As effective as word of mouth is, you can't build a brand by mouth alone. You have got to give that first mouth something to work with. Unfortunately, too many companies use Internet brand names that are unspeakable. And many others are common names that discourage word-of-mouth usage.

Daewoo Daihatsu Suzuki

Daewoo, Daihatsu, and Suzuki are three Asian automobile brands that have never done well in the American market. One reason: Their names are difficult to pronounce and difficult to spell.

"Where did you buy your new computer?"

"It was Onsale."

"I know you got a good deal, but where?"

"Onsale."

Onsale.com might be a difficult name to use in ordinary conversation, but many other Websites are even worse. They're also hard to pronounce and spell. Some examples: Entrepreneur.com, Concierge.com, Cyberluxury.com, Onvia.com, imandi.com, Brodia.com, iWon.com, iOwn.com, Richoshet.com, zUniversity.com, Shabang.com, uBid.com, Cozone.com, GiftEmporia.com, iParty.com, eHow.com, Travelocity.com, Adornis.com, 2Key.com.

When someone recommends a physical brand or a real-world retail store, you don't have to remember exactly how to spell the name in order to find the store. Is it Abercrombie & Fitch or Abacromby & Finch? It doesn't matter in the mall; it does matter on the Web.

That's why an Internet brand should always try to line up all possible spelling variations of its name. 2Key and TwoKey, for example.

(Roughly 10 percent of the buying public suffers from some form of dyslexia. Why write off—or rather, spell off—the dyslexia market?)

Another problem is the mixing of letters and numbers. Very few outernet brands use both. (We could think of only 3M, 3Com, and 1-800-FLOWERS.)

Quite a few Internet brands, on the other hand, make this mistake: 1stBuy.com, 123greetings.com, 123tel.com, How2.com, Net2phonedirect.com, Pop2it.com, Click2Asia.com, Shop2give.com, MP3.com, 4anything.com, 4charity.com, Fax4Free.com, Opus360.com, 800.com, 911gifts.com.

Why do most people find it easier to remember their phone number than their license plate number, even though they are both about the same length? Because license plates usually use both numbers and letters, which makes them much more difficult to recall. While the combination can

Kids don't have to know how to spell "Abercrombie & Fitch" in order to patronize this hot chain of stores. The Internet is different. You have to know the exact spelling or you won't be able to reach the site.

sometimes make cute vanity plates (321GO), they make poor brand names.

And did you ever try to remember a Canadian postal code like H3B 2Y7? A mixture of letters and numbers is usually much harder to recall than either letters or numbers alone.

One of the reasons that companies select unspeakable brand names has to do with the selection process.

Most brand names are selected visually, usually from a list of names printed on oversized sheets of white paper pasted on cardboard.

That's not the way prospects deal with brand names. They usually hear them verbally from friends, neighbors, relatives, and coworkers. Even the media exposure of brand names is heavily weighted to verbal rather than visual media. Nearly 90 percent of the average person's media time is spent listening to radio or television versus less than 10 percent reading newspapers or magazines.

In case you're wondering, the words you hear in a television commercial are far more likely to make an impression in your mind than the words you read on the screen. (The spoken word conveys emotion and secondary meanings, while the printed word just sits emotionless on the page or on the TV screen.)

When you select a brand name, you should listen to the proposed name being spoken, and not just stare at the word on a board. You can't hear capital letters or the sound of a circle ®. To be effective, a brand name needs to sound like a proper name or a word that conjures up a particular Website, not just a generic category.

7. THE NAME SHOULD BE SHOCKING.

If you want prospects to remember your Internet brand, you need to make the name itself "shocking."

The best brand names have always had an element of shock or surprise. DieHard, the largest selling automobile

Younger people are usually more tolerant of "shocking" names like FUBU, which has become a successful hip-hop fashion brand. (FUBU stands for "For Us, By Us.")

battery, for example. Häagen-Dazs, the leading premium ice cream. Diesel, the fashionable brand of jeans.

It's easy to go overboard and make the name so shocking that it offends people. FUBU is a brand name that comes close to the edge, although younger people are usually more tolerant of truly shocking names.

People sometimes ask us why we call our laws "immutable." Aren't some of your laws mutable? Maybe so, we reply, but to make it in the book business you need a shocking title. *The 22 Generally Accepted Laws of Branding* is just not going to go anywhere at Barnes & Noble, Borders, or Amazon.com.

One of the most difficult tasks in public relations is getting a business book reviewed in the media. We're going to try as hard as possible, but the odds are that this book will probably be the eighth book we have written that will not be reviewed by the *Wall Street Journal*.

But the *Journal* did review a book entitled *Leadership Secrets of Attila the Hun*. Four hundred years from now, will the 25th-century *Wall Street Journal* review a digital book entitled *Leadership Secrets of Adolf Hitler*? Could be.

An element of "shock" makes a name more memorable because it puts the power of emotion to work. To a certain extent, you remember events in your own life based on the degree of emotional involvement. Your graduation day, your wedding day, the day John F. Kennedy was shot, the day the Twin Towers were destroyed.

You may have taken dozens of vacations in your lifetime, most of which remain in your mind as fuzzy memories. The vacations you will never forget, however, are the ones that contain strong emotional elements. An automobile accident, an overturned sailboat, the day you stepped on a sea urchin.

You see the same pattern on the Internet. Common names like Cooking.com and Furniture.com are bland and carry no shock or emotional involvement. They're hard to remember.

It's names that have a bit of bite to them that will turn out to be the better brand names on the Internet. Names like

If you want to write a successful book, make sure the title is "shocking." *Leadership Secrets of Attila the Hun* is a good example.

Go is a short, simple name for a Disney portal that allows you to explore the wonders of the Web. But it's not nearly as memorable as Yahoo!. Recently Disney scrapped its highly promoted Go.com Website and took a write-off of more that $800 million. Meanwhile, Yahoo! continues to make money.

Yahoo! and Amazon.com. These are names that stir up some emotional response.

One good branding strategy for any Internet company is to immediately lock the "shocking" name into both the category and the benefit. Amazon.com has promoted itself as "Earth's biggest bookstore." This strategy works on several levels. The Amazon is the Earth's "biggest" river, and the alliteration of "biggest bookstore" makes the phrase more memorable.

If you don't lock your shocking name into either a category or a benefit, you waste the power of the name. We always thought that Prodigy was a good name for an Internet service provider, but not for a general site. Prodigy, in our opinion, should have been directed at children.

Other memorable names are MotleyFool and EarthLink. (Although when Earthlink acquired MindSpring, it should have used the MindSpring name, which is more shocking.) Also memorable because they are shocking are Hotmail, the most popular free e-mail service, and Monster.com, the leading Website for job listings.

8. THE NAME SHOULD BE PERSONALIZED.

Obviously, every Internet brand cannot accommodate all of these eight naming strategies, including personalization. But when the situation allows it, you should consider naming your site after an individual.

This strategy has a number of advantages. First of all, it assures you a Website with a proper name rather than a common name. Second, it enhances the publicity potential of your site.

Many real-world brands have evolved from individuals. Ford, Chrysler, Chevrolet, Pontiac, Olds(mobile), Buick, Cadillac, Calvin Klein, Ralph Lauren, Tommy Hilfiger, Donna Karan, Liz Claiborne, L.L. Bean, Boeing, Forbes, Goodyear, Gillette, Heinz, Hertz, and Orville Redenbacher, to name a few.

Initially Dell Computer sold its products under the PC

Limited brand name. But ultimately the company realized that the proper name (Dell) was much stronger than the generic name (PC Limited), so it switched.

You enhance the publicity potential of a brand when you use the founder's name as the brand name. Look at all the publicity Michael Dell has received, publicity that directly benefits the brand. His competitor Mr. Compaq seldom gets mentioned.

And where would the Trump brands be without The Donald? Nowhere, because Donald doesn't like to spend money when he can get something for free. Don't knock PR. Donald Trump's whirlwind activities on behalf of his brands are what has made them successful.

Brands are cold, silent, and lifeless. Only a person can articulate the brand's strategy, position, and objectives. The media want to interview people, not brands. And whenever possible, the media want to interview the CEO, not the brand manager.

Relax and enjoy it. If you are the CEO and you want your brand to become famous, you have to become famous, too. The most famous brands usually also have celebrity CEOs. Microsoft and Bill Gates. Sun Microsystems and Scott McNealey. Oracle and Larry Ellison. Apple and Steve Jobs.

Same on the Internet. AOL and Steve Case. Amazon.com and Jeff Bezos. Yahoo! and Jerry Yang and David Filo.

Simplify things. Make it easy for both your prospects and the media to associate the chief executive with the Website. Give them both the same name.

- Donald Trump and Trump.com

- Michael Dell and Dell.com

- Charles Schwab and Schwab.com

All branding work starts with the name. If you pick a name that matches most of these eight naming strategies, then you will be well on your way to building a successful Internet brand.

In 1999, Papa John's Pizza passed Little Caesars to become the third largest pizza chain in the United States. The publicity generated by John Schnatter, the papa of Papa John's, is a major reason for the success of the chain.

There's a special section of the business hall of fame for those people who manage to make the covers of both *Time* and *Newsweek* magazines, as Donald Trump did.

5 THE LAW OF SINGULARITY

At all costs you should avoid being
second in your category.

There's one big difference between branding on the Internet
and branding in the real world.

In the real world, there is always room for a number two
brand.

- Duracell and Energizer

- Kodak and Fuji

- Hertz and Avis

- Nike and Reebok

- Goodyear and Michelin

There's a reason why number two brands can lead a
healthy life on the outernet. They serve a need, not just for
the consumer, but also for the trade.

Would a supermarket just stock Coca-Cola and not a
second brand? No. The second brand gives the supermarket
some leverage against the leader. "If Coca-Cola won't partici-
pate in our weekly promotion, we'll ask Pepsi-Cola."

The unspoken implication of every request made by the
trade is, if you turn this deal down, we'll offer it to your competitor. The number two brand fills a real need for the trade.

Would airline terminal management sign an exclusive

deal with Hertz, the leading car rental brand? Not if they wanted to have some leverage on the number of cars available for rent, the hours of service, the pricing, and so forth.

Say there's a McDonald's on the corner of a highly desirable fast-food site. The real-estate developer across the street can't sell the site to Mickey D, so he or she turns to Burger King.

The airline terminal, the supermarket, the drugstore, the mall operator, even the real-estate developer—all come between the customer and the brand. These middlemen, or the trade if you will, have a strong need for number two brands, even if the number two brand is essentially the same. It's not a product need. It's a leverage need.

You find a similar need in the industrial field; most companies insist on "a second source of supply." What if their primary supplier is out on strike? If a company didn't have a second source of supply for a particular part, it might have to shut down its production line.

"Nothing comes between me and my Calvins," Brooke Shields once said. On the Internet nothing comes between the customer and the brand. There are no middlemen, no trade, no real estate developers, no need for leverage against the leader. It's what Bill Gates calls "friction-free capitalism."

As a result, the Internet is more like a football game or a political contest. It's the Law of Singularity. Second place is no place.

Or as a Nike television commercial once said about the Olympics, "you don't win silver, you lose gold." On the Internet, there are no silver or bronze medals.

On the Internet, monopolies will rule. There is no room on the Internet for number-two brands. The Internet will operate more like the computer software industry, in which every category tends to be dominated by a single brand.

- In PC operating systems, it's Windows.

- In PC word-processing software, it's Word.

- In PC spreadsheet software, it's Excel.

Dannon and Yoplait dominate the yogurt category. In virtually every product category, you will find two major brands.

In job listings, Monster.com is flying high over all the other career-related Websites in the field. "We have over 50 percent market share in almost every category," says CEO Jeff Taylor.

- In PC presentation software, it's PowerPoint.
- In PC accounting software, it's Quicken.
- In PC tax-preparation software, it's TurboTax.

Michael Mauboussin, chief investment strategist at Credit Suisse First Boston, found that Internet sites adhere to a mathematical valuation system so rigid, it resembles patterns found in nature. The pattern suggests that there may be fewer ultimate winners than many investors expect.

As some sites get bigger, Mr. Mauboussin argues, they attract more users, and the more users they attract, the richer and more useful they become, attracting more users. This produces a "winner-take-all" outcome: a handful of Websites with almost all the business, and the rest with next to nothing; i.e., the Law of Singularity.

One of the many advantages of friction-free retailing is that there is no one in between the customer and the manufacturer taking a cut of the transaction. The price you pay for the lack of friction, however, is the virtual disappearance of the second brand.

For many products, it's the retailer that is responsible for the strength of the second brand. No retailer wants to be totally dependent on a single brand in each category. To do so would be to put the retailer at the mercy of the manufacturer. The second brand keeps the first brand honest.

For the most part, there seems to be a cordial relationship between manufacturers and retailers, but despite the surface friendliness, there are often deep disagreements about prices, payment terms, stocking fees, co-op advertising allowances, and return privileges. In the retail world, you don't fight fire with fire. You fight fire with a second brand.

On the Web the situation is different. The real world is the second brand. When Amazon.com offers best-sellers at 40 percent off, the book buyer mentally compares the Amazon deal with the 30 percent off one can find at most brick-and-mortar bookstores.

When Barnesandnoble.com (now bn.com) says "me, too," the prospect yawns. There just isn't any reason to switch, unless Amazon.com suffers a breakdown in service or pricing.

There's another reason why the Web puts the second brand under pressure. In the physical world, one brand's success creates a trend in the opposite direction. This is especially true for a fashion-oriented brand.

"No one goes there anymore," said Yogi Berra. "It's getting too popular." Not as many people wear Ralph Lauren anymore either; it was getting too popular. Now a lot of folks are into Tommy Hilfiger.

If it's Tommy today, you can be sure that tomorrow it will be somebody totally different. That's the power of the second-brand approach.

But the Web lacks the visibility of the physical world. If everyone bought their books from Amazon.com, how would you know? It's this lack of visibility that mutes the backlash against a brand leader.

In reality, of course, there are many second brands on the Internet. Not only seconds, but thirds, fourths, fifths, and even sixths. In furniture for example, we have Behome.com, Decoratewithstyle.com, Dwr.com, Furniture.com, Furniture-Find.com, Furnitureonline.com, HomeDecorators.com, HomePortfolio.com, Housenet.com, Living.com, and many more that we don't know about.

Does this mean that the furniture category is different from books? That the furniture category might have many brands, but that the book category will be dominated by one brand, presumably Amazon.com?

Not at all. It only means that there is no clear-cut furniture leader today. But tomorrow is another matter. In all likelihood, one furniture brand will get out in front of the pack and go on to dominate the category. What happened in books is likely to happen in furniture.

History sheds some light on this process. In 1910, there

| Calvin Klein |
| Ralph Lauren |
| Tommy Hilfiger |

In the fashion field, no brand lives forever. First it was Calvin Klein. Then Ralph Lauren knocked out Calvin. Currently Tommy Hilfiger is making inroads against Ralph.

were 508 American automobile companies. Today there are just two: General Motors and Ford.

In 1985, there were almost a hundred companies making disk drives. Today, two companies, Quantum and Seagate, dominate the disk-drive market on a worldwide basis.

In 1990, there were some two hundred companies making personal computers. Today, two brands (Compaq and Dell) dominate the category.

In the real world, we call this process "the law of duality." In the long run, two brands will dominate the category, putting the third brand under enormous pressure.

- Compaq and Dell dominate the personal-computer market, putting the IBM brand under pressure. IBM, which was losing millions on personal computers, recently announced that they would withdraw from the retail market.

- Coca-Cola and Pepsi-Cola dominate the cola market, putting the squeeze on the Royal Crown brand. RC Cola has been steadily losing market share.

- Kodak and Fuji dominate the photographic film market, virtually shutting out Agfa and driving the brand off most shelves.

It doesn't get any better for a brand buried in the pack. As time goes on, opportunities disappear. The leaders become more fixed in their positions. The longer a brand remains an also-ran, the less likely it is to catch up.

Substitute "singularity" for duality and you have a long-term picture of the Internet. Friction-free retailing has eliminated the function of the second brand.

Take books, for example. Will either Borders.com or bn.com overtake Amazon.com? Unlikely, unless Amazon.com makes a major mistake.

Will either Borders.com or bn.com close the gap with Amazon.com? That's unlikely, too. What is far more likely to happen is that Amazon.com will increase its share of the online book

In the orange juice category, Citrus Hill was a weak number-three brand behind Tropicana and Minute Maid. Yet Procter & Gamble thought it could use its marketing muscle to make Citrus Hill a leader. After a decade of losses, P&G finally threw in the towel and killed the brand. In marketing, number three is usually nowhere.

market, putting severe pressure on both Borders.com and bn.com. The law of singularity at work.

But stay tuned. Amazon.com is in the process of making that major mistake that will open the door for its book competitors (see the Law of Vanity).

Is there any hope for a brand buried in second place? Of course there is. But the highest form of strategic thinking is to first look at your situation with a cold eye.

The impossible is impossible. If it's going to be impossible to make progress head-on against an Amazon.com, then you must back off and try a different approach.

What might that approach be? If the laws of branding are immutable (and we think they are), then you must do exactly the same thing that Amazon.com did. You must be first in a new category.

You can always create an opportunity to be first in a new category by narrowing your focus and by appealing to a segment of the market. It's as simple as that.

Instead of duplicating Amazon.com's site, a better strategy for bn.com would have been to narrow the focus and specialize in a category of books. Business books, for example.

Which brings up the Law of Either/Or. If the Web was going to be a business for Borders and Barnes & Noble, then they would have needed different names on their Websites. With the same names, it is harder to create identities on the Web that are distinct and different from their identities in the physical world. Line extension strikes again.

Actually a number of Internet companies are trying to compete with Amazon.com by doing exactly as we have just suggested, by narrowing their focus.

- Alibris.com in the used-book category.

- Medsite.com in the medical-book category.

- Varsitybooks.com in the textbook category.

Borders.com

After years of losses, the Borders Group, the nation's second-largest bookseller, decided to close its online store and have Amazon.com serve its customers instead.

In automobiles, Mercedes-Benz owns the "prestige" category, but by introducing smaller, less expensive vehicles is in danger of losing its position.

In each of these categories, of course, there are a number of other Internet brands. So which brand will be the winner in each category? It won't necessarily be the brand that was first in the marketplace. It won't necessarily be the brand that was first to become profitable. The winner will be the first brand to establish a dominant position in the prospect's mind. Then the Law of Singularity will take over and dampen the market shares of the runners-up. Nothing succeeds like success.

When building an Internet brand, you have to think category first and brand second. Customers are not primarily interested in companies, in brands, or even in Websites. They are primarily interested in categories. They are not primarily interested in buying a Volvo, for example. They buy a Volvo in order to get a safe car. Volvo is the leader in a mental category called "safe cars."

What's a Chevrolet? In truth, a Chevrolet is a large, small, cheap, expensive car or truck. One reason for the continuing decline of Chevrolet sales is the fact that General Motors has neglected to define the mental category that Chevrolet is supposed to occupy.

If you want to be the leader in a category, you first have to tell the prospect what the category is. Take a two-page advertisement from a recent issue of the *Harvard Business Review*. There were only fifteen words in the entire ad and here is every one of them.

> The internet is a blank canvas.
>
> You hold the brush.
>
> intendchange.com
>
> intendchange
>
> image · build · reinvent

Will the reader of this Intendchange.com advertisement have any idea what the category is? We doubt it. Which might be one reason the Website folded in July 2000. It never hurts to tell the reader exactly where to file your brand name in the mind. Books, auctions, whatever.

"Earth's biggest bookstore" not only stakes out a category for Amazon.com, but also makes a strong claim for leadership in the category. "Image, build, reinvent" does neither.

In summary, don't get discouraged if you're not the dominant brand in a category. Just channel your branding efforts in a different direction. Just narrow your focus.

You can always create a powerful brand by narrowing the focus on the leader. The Internet is an enormous medium. The opportunities to narrow the focus are astronomical.

In the real world, many narrowly focused brands have been extraordinarily successful in competing with market leaders.

Back in the early eighties, IBM was the most powerful company in the world. It made the most money and had the best reputation. IBM was also the first company to introduce a serious 16-bit office personal computer, the IBM PC. So is IBM the leader in PCs today? No, Dell Computer is.

Unlike IBM, Dell made only one product (personal computers) marketed to one segment (the business community) and sold through one distribution channel (direct to customers). Yet today Dell outsells all other competitors in personal computers. Less often yields much more.

What Dell did in personal computers, Sun Microsystems did in workstations. By focusing on UNIX workstations, Sun built a powerful brand and a profitable company. You don't have to have a full line to be successful.

When the Web matures, of course, there will be opportunities for number-two brands. Until that day arrives, you need to be the leading brand in your category or look for an opportunity to narrow the focus in order to create a new category you can be the leader in.

All the major computer manufacturers sell storage, including IBM, Sun, and Compaq, but the leader in information storage is not any of the computer giants, it's the specialist, EMC. They call themselves "the storage architects."

6 THE LAW OF INTERNET ADVERTISING

Advertising off the Net will be a lot bigger than advertising on the Net.

Death and taxes used to be the only certainties in life. Today you can add one more: advertising.

Advertising messages are ubiquitous. Everywhere you turn you'll find an advertising message. From television to taxicabs to T-shirts. From billboards to buses to bathrooms. (Now you can't even take a leak without being exposed to advertising.) In some circles, elevators are considered the next fast-rising advertising medium.

Every major auto race, golf tournament, and tennis tournament has a corporate sponsor. All the bowl games are already taken, from the Hooters Hula Bowl in Hawaii to the AT&T Rose Bowl in Pasadena to the Nokia Sugar Bowl in New Orleans.

Sports arenas around the country are rapidly selling their names for advertising purposes. In San Francisco, Candlestick Park is now 3Com Stadium. The Washington Redskins' Landover Stadium is now FedEx Field. Internet companies are also getting into the act. The Baltimore Ravens sold the naming rights for their National Football League stadium to PSINet in a twenty-year deal for $105 million.

But the mother of all naming deals happened in Atlanta. Naming rights for the city's new basketball and hockey stadium were sold to Philips NV in a package deal estimated to be worth $200 million over twenty years. (The new Philips Arena cost only $140.5 million to build.)

When the name on the stadium is worth more than the physical stadium itself, you know that we live in an advertising-oriented world.

The traditional media, of course, have been saturated with advertising for as long as we can remember.

The average magazine is 60 percent advertising. The average newspaper is 70 percent advertising. But print media are at least partially supported by subscribers. Radio and broadcast television are almost totally supported by the advertising revenues they generate.

And they generate a lot of revenue. In a recent year, advertisers spent $49 billion on broadcast TV advertising and $17 billion on radio advertising.

Cable television was once touted as the first ad-free communications medium, but that didn't last very long. Today cable TV is almost as saturated with advertising as regular TV.

With billions and billions of advertising dollars chasing every available medium, you can't blame the Internet folks for trying to tap into this treasure trove. The Internet was going to be another advertising medium, but bigger and better and eventually more rewarding than television.

Initially, at least, advertising supported all the commercial Websites. The game plan was simple: "We will give away the content in order to draw traffic, which we can then use to sell advertising." Exactly the way television and radio currently work.

So we had free browsers, free search engines, free electronic mail, free electronic greeting cards, free Internet access. Even free phone calls and free tax returns.

Instead of paying America Online $23.90 a month, you used to be able to sign up with NetZero and get ten hours of Internet service per month for nothing. The catch: You had to

Free-PC created an avalanche of publicity when it offered a free computer in return for the user's willingness to accept advertising messages on the screen. They were quickly followed by many other sites offering a wide variety of free services. Most of these ventures are now dead in the water. Headline of a recent front-page article in *The New York Times:* "Free Rides Are Now Passé on Information Highway."

Win $1 billion at Grab.com

The ultimate giveaway happened on December 27, 2000, when Grab.com gave away $1 billion. Rather, it didn't happen, because no one picked the right numbers. This was not too surprising, since the odds of winning were 1 in 2.4 billion.

fill out a questionnaire that revealed your demographic information and agree to put up with an onslaught of advertising messages. (Today NetZero has merged with Juno and changed its name to United Online, and it charges $9.95 a month.)

There was even free beer on the Net. Miller Brewing gave away two million electronic coupons each good for one six-pack of any Miller beer brand.

The great Internet giveaway reached its zenith when a company called Free-PC announced a plan to give away ten thousand Compaq computers that permanently display on-screen ads. More than a million people volunteered to take one.

If "free" isn't a big enough come-on, how about "pay"? A number of Websites offered to pay you for exposing yourself to advertising while you surfed the Net.

AllAdvantage.com offered to pay you fifty cents an hour (up to ten hours a month). MyPoints.com gave you either cash or points that could be exchanged for things like free movie rentals, gift certificates, ski-lift tickets, even exotic vacations. (Surf the Web today, surf Hawaii tomorrow.)

Many Websites featured giveaways of one kind or another. PlanetRx.com gave away 672 Palm V organizers (one an hour, every day, for four weeks). Lycos.com is a portal that had a Lucky Numbers Game you could play up to four times a day. Just pick six numbers and cross your fingers. You could have won one of 5,000 prizes, including a grand prize of $5 million.

The really big money was being thrown around by the CBS-backed Website iWon.com. The portal was giving away $10,000 a day, $1 million a month, and a cool $10 million on tax day, April 15, 2000. (Get it? I won.)

What the giveaway had to do with the Website remains a mystery. Unlike Youbet.com, iWon.com is not a gambling site. Rather, it is a portal that offers e-mail, search services, and online shopping, as well as content from CBS Websites including SportsLine USA and MarketWatch.com. All financed with $100 million of CBS money.

Besides the giveaways, many sites spent a fortune on

launch parties. Pixelon.com, a California company that planned to introduce a new Internet-broadcast technology, raised $23 million of venture capital and then promptly spent $10 million of that on a launch party. Called iBash '99, the day-long Las Vegas party was headlined by The Who, along with other acts that included Kiss, Natalie Cole, the Dixie Chicks, Tony Bennett, and LeAnn Rimes.

It won't surprise you to learn that Pixelon.com is no longer with us. It did surprise the investors, however, when they found out that the founder was a convicted con artist and a fugitive from the law.

This flurry of spending was designed to attract millions of Web visitors who could then be sold off to companies as advertising chattel. As a matter of fact, Internet operators were drooling over the advertising riches soon to fall their way. Forrester Research, a high-tech consulting firm, predicted that advertising spending on the Internet would jump from $2 billion in 1999 to $22 billion in 2004, or 8 percent of total spending. This would mean that the Internet passed the magazine medium and was neck and neck with radio.

Don't believe a word of it. The Internet would be the first new medium that will not be dominated by advertising.

Let us repeat that statement. The Internet will be the first new medium that will not be dominated by advertising, and the reason is simple.

The Internet is interactive. For the first time, the user is in charge, not the owner of the medium. The user can decide where to go, what to look at, and what to read. At many sites, the user can decide how to pick and arrange the material to best fit that user's needs.

Advertising is not something that people look forward to. They tend to have an underlying resentment toward advertising. They see it as an intrusion into their space, an invasion of their privacy. "Junk mail" is the popular term for direct-mail advertising.

(If magazines were interactive, the first thing readers

Click rate: 0.3%

The click rate for Internet banner ads continues to fall. Currently it is a measly 0.3 percent.

would do is to put all the editorial material up front and all the advertising in the back.)

Initially, of course, people were curious about this new medium called the Internet. And they were happy to click on banner ads to see what the buzz was all about.

But things are changing. Surveys show that the number of people who click on Internet ads has been dropping steadily. According to Nielsen/NetRatings, which tracks the effectiveness of Internet advertising, the click rate in two years dropped from 1.35 percent to 0.3 percent.

Internet advertising rates have also been dropping, not a sign of a healthy medium. According to one research firm, the cost for banner ads has dropped from $20 per thousand last year to about $10 per thousand this year.

For a number of years, the largest advertiser on the Internet has been General Motors, which is currently spending about $50 million a year on Web advertising, or about 2 percent of its annual advertising budget. (All this advertising didn't help GM much. Its share of the domestic automobile market has declined to 27 percent, its lowest level since the thirties.)

One indication of the user's attitude toward Internet advertising is the rapid rise of ad-blocking software. Known by names like At Guard, Junkbuster Proxy, Intermute, and Web Washer, these programs work by blocking ads before they appear on the user's screen. Often they speed up computer performance because they skip the files that contain ads loaded with graphics, making page loading far quicker.

Even the $3 billion of current Internet advertising is a dubious number. It includes commissions paid to such companies as Doubleclick, the leading seller of advertising on the Net.

Doubleclick is aptly named. Instead of the traditional advertising agency's 15 percent commission, Doubleclick takes 35 percent to 50 percent of the Internet advertising it sells. Maybe Tripleclick would be a more appropriate name.

Not all Internet advertising revenues represent real

Advertising: The Holy Grail

The *Wall Street Journal* recently reported that "advertising remains the Web's Holy Grail: everyone in the business knows it's out there, if only some site can figure out a way to convince advertisers that its 'unique' Web visitors are focusing on those little winken-and-blinken ad icons." It might be churlish of us to mention that they never found the real Holy Grail either.

money either. Some sites swap advertising with each other, allowing each dotcom to book ad revenues. (The kid who trades a $50,000 dog for two $25,000 cats isn't really receiving $50,000 in revenue.)

Don't be misled either by the apparent analogies with the print and broadcast media. The Internet is not just another medium. If it were, it would not be the revolutionary medium that many people, including us, believe it is going to be. As such, you should expect to see a revolution, not just a replay of the past.

Was television a revolutionary new medium? Not really. Did it change your life in any significant way? Not really. Even television's highly touted home shopping networks didn't amount to very much. "Radio with pictures" was the judgment of many commentators.

You can't have it both ways. The Internet cannot be a revolutionary new medium that operates in exactly the same way as traditional media. Where's the revolution?

It's staring us in the face. The Internet is interactive, and that's the revolutionary aspect of the medium. For the first time the target is in charge, not the shooter. And what the target definitely does not want is more advertising arrows shot in its direction.

What people do want is information. Prices, sizes, weights, shipping dates, product comparisons. All presented in an interactive format.

We're not negative about advertising. Quite the contrary. The Internet will continue to spawn an enormous increase in advertising volume, except that it will be off the Net rather than on the Net. This advertising will be "tune-in"— or rather "type-in"—advertising that will direct you to the names of specific Internet sites.

For a couple of years, the Internet drove up advertising on the outernet, especially on radio and television. Radio, in particular, was red-hot, with three years of double-digit increases in a row.

Then the dotcom disaster hit, followed by the terrorist attacks, and all advertising expenditures are down. But we expect that as the economy improves, advertising volume will increase, with dotcoms making a strong comeback.

Super Bowl Sunday was a particular favorite of Internet advertisers. Of the 36 companies that bought advertising time on Super Bowl XXXIV, 17, or almost half, were dotcoms. The NFL extravaganza didn't come cheap, either. The average cost for a thirty-second commercial was more than $2 million, an increase of 25 percent over Super Bowl XXXIII.

The reason the Internet has resulted in dramatic increases in outernet advertising has to do with the nature of the human mind.

One of the most remarkable characteristics of the human mind is its ability to forget.

Some things, of course, are never forgotten. A cruel insult in high school. Getting dumped by a lover. Being fired from a job. It all depends on the emotional impact of the event.

A person who can remember all the details of an embarrassing event that happened several decades ago might easily forget the underwear brand he or she put on this morning.

An Internet brand suffers from this ability of the mind to forget in two different ways. First, the brand is invisible on a daily basis. Many brands in the physical world benefit from a daily dose of visual reinforcement. Shell, Starbucks, Mobil, Coca-Cola, McDonald's, Tylenol. There are literally thousands of brands that a person will regularly see on the highways, in the supermarkets, in the drugstores.

An Internet brand, on the other hand, will never suddenly appear before you unless you summon it to do so. Out of sight, out of mind.

Second, an Internet brand (like most brands) suffers from a lack of emotional involvement. Some people fall in love with their brands. Most do not.

For most people a brand is nothing more than a guarantee

Every day, a retail brand like Starbucks generates millions of visual impressions on customers and prospects. An Internet brand suffers from this lack of daily visual reinforcement.

of quality and a system for saving time. A way of making sure that the products you buy are decent without having to spend an inordinate amount of time comparing one product with another. Not too many people fall in love with a bottle of Heinz ketchup. Which is why Heinz needs the visibility on supermarket shelves and restaurant tables to keep the brand alive.

What does an Internet brand need to do to stay alive? It also needs visibility in the real, or physical, world.

The best and most cost-effective way to achieve visibility is with publicity. The first brand in a new Internet category is generally blessed by a blizzard of publicity. Amazon.com, Priceline.com, and Bluemountain.com are prime examples.

Some sites are capable of generating publicity on a continuing basis. The crazy auctions that happen every day on eBay are an endless source of stories. A recent headline in the *National Enquirer:* "He buys $3 pickle jar at garage sale & sells it for $44,000." (On eBay, naturally.)

The Internet itself will spawn an enormous increase in PR activity. "Just as network TV built the advertising business," says Ray Gaulke, former president of the Public Relations Society of America, "the Internet technology has the capacity to dramatically build the PR business."

Sooner or later, however, many Internet brands will exhaust their publicity potential. At this point they will need to shift their emphasis from publicity to advertising. How else are you going to keep an invisible Internet brand alive?

Publicity first, advertising second is the general rule, and it applies to all branding programs, especially for Internet brands. (A much more detailed discussion of the relationship between publicity and advertising is contained in this book under the Law of Publicity and the Law of Advertising.)

As the Internet grows up, you are going to see an explosion in outernet advertising. And much of this advertising will be directed at creating customers for Internet brands.

In particular, radio will turn out to be the primary

Powerful Internet brands like Amazon, Yahoo!, eBay, and others were built by massive doses of publicity. Advertising played only a minor role in their success.

Radio, the invisible medium, is the perfect partner for the Net, also an invisible medium. Using radio to advertise your Internet brand forces you to focus on the verbal aspects of your site. If Pets.com had used radio instead of television, it would never have launched the disastrous Sock Puppet campaign.

medium for dotcom advertising. Radio's perceived negative, the lack of visuals, is not a disadvantage for an Internet brand. There are no visual attributes of an Internet brand. No yellow flesh that helps identify Perdue chicken. No radiator grills that do the same for Mercedes-Benz automobiles. The only thing your mind needs to remember to log on to a site is the name.

On the Internet the name is everything. A verbal medium like radio is perfect for driving an Internet name into the mind. Advertising might be vitally important for driving prospects to your site, but once they get there you can forget about using them as human fodder for your advertising messages.

On the Internet, interactivity is king. Advertising is something that prospects put up with, not something they search out. Interactivity gives them a choice, and in our opinion most people will use this choice to turn off the advertising and turn on the information.

If you want to build a brand on the Net, forget about trying to attract advertising to your Website.

Make your brand a source of information that prospects cannot find elsewhere. Or a place to buy things they cannot find elsewhere. Or a place to buy things at prices they cannot find elsewhere. Or a place to meet people they cannot meet elsewhere.

Don't make your site an excuse to run advertising that people have already seen in newspapers and magazines or heard on radio or TV.

The Internet is a revolutionary new interactive medium. And when people interact with advertising, they generally turn it off.

7　THE LAW OF GLOBALISM

The Internet will demolish all barriers,
all boundaries, all borders.

One of the major factors driving the global economy of the nineties was the collapse of communism in the late eighties. Instead of a world divided into armed camps, everybody was suddenly in the same boat.

Instead of trading insults, the major countries of the globe started to trade products and services.

But what caused the fall of communism? In our opinion, it wasn't the massive military buildup in the West, although that might have been necessary for defensive purposes. In our opinion, it was television.

If you visited the USSR before its fall, you know that the population was under intense publicity pressure to believe that everything was superior in the Union of Socialist Soviet Republics. Free health care, jobs for all, housing for everybody.

To the outsider, it wasn't true. There were a lot of rubles, but nothing to buy, as one look at the mostly empty shelves in the stores would have told you. Not to mention the long line whenever a store got a shipment of a desirable item.

Soviet authorities, of course, blocked Western newspapers and magazines from crossing their borders, but they couldn't block Western television signals.

Television brought truth to the Soviet people. When they

Globalism

"An invasion of armies can be resisted," wrote Victor Hugo, "but not an idea whose time has come." All the protests in the world will not stop the arrival of the global business community. And the Internet is the catalyst that is making it happen.

were able to see the profusion of goods and services in the Western countries, they lost their faith in communism.

"The medium is the message" is the famous dictum of Marshall McLuhan. If you define "message" simply as "content" or "information," McLuhan pointed out, you miss one of the most important features of any medium: its power to change the course and functioning of human relations and activities.

The message of the television medium was "capitalism." As long as the Soviet Union was infiltrated by television signals from the West, there was no way to keep communism alive. It had to give way to a market-driven economy based on a free-enterprise system. TV literally helped change the course of human history.

What is the "message" of the Internet medium? We believe the message is "globalism." Ultimately, the Internet will drive the citizens of the world into one interconnected global economy. "The global village," in Marshall McLuhan's vocabulary.

It may well be that the biggest trend of the twenty-first century will turn out to be globalism. What the Internet hath wrought is the global village. The medium, after all, is the message.

America, with 59 percent of all homes connected, is the dominant dog in Internet usage. Thirty-six percent of the world's Internet population lives in the United States. But there are other countries where Internet usage is actually higher. Canada has 60 percent of all homes connected. Sweden has 65 percent. If our domestic experience is any guide, usage should explode in every developed country of the world. When that happens, the world will become one big global marketplace.

The potential is awesome. America is by far the largest economy in the world with the greatest output of goods and services and the highest standard of living. Yet the United

States accounts for less than 5 percent of the world's population, a percentage that declines annually.

If you're a businessperson in America, where does the real opportunity lie? In the domestic market or in the 95 percent of the world that doesn't live in one of the fifty states?

Obviously the global market is going to be far more important than the domestic market to the success of almost every American company. It won't happen overnight, but it will happen.

There's a long way to go. Currently the United States exports only 11 percent of its gross domestic product. (It also exports capital to other countries, where the money is used to build plants, distribution systems, and most important of all, brands.)

What makes the American economic system so globally powerful is not the physical products or the plants or the systems, it's the brands themselves: Microsoft, Intel, Dell, Cisco, Coca-Cola, Hertz. These and other American brands dominate a host of categories on the worldwide scene.

This is not a one-way street, however. The Internet is not just an opportunity to export American brands and American cultures overseas. The opposite is also likely to happen. It's already happened in many categories.

- While McDonald's has carried American fast food around the world, the truth is that a large number of Americans are eating Italian, Mexican, Chinese, French, and Japanese food.

- While Disney has just signed a deal for a new theme park in Hong Kong, the truth is that the most popular characters among the kiddie crowd in America are not Mickey Mouse or Donald Duck. They're Pokémon characters from Japan.

- Starbucks is a European-style coffee house blended with an American brand name.

PricewaterhouseCoopers
KPMG
Deloitte Touche Tohmatsu
Ernst & Young
Andersen

The Big 5 accounting firms dominate the tax and audit business on a worldwide basis. The same phenomenon has occurred in many other businesses, including advertising, computers, software, distilled spirits, etc.

Rolex is a Swiss brand of expensive watches that has established an enviable position in virtually every country in the world.

- Evian from France started the trend toward branded bottled water, which has become an enormous category in the United States.

- Volkswagen from Germany and Toyota from Japan started the trend toward small cars in America.

- Mercedes-Benz and BMW from Germany started the trend toward small ultraluxury cars in the U.S.

- At the high end of the market, wine from France, watches from Switzerland, and clothing from Italy have had a major impact in the American market.

America has always been a melting pot for people, but it has also become a melting pot for products from around the world. With the rise of the Internet, that trend is going to accelerate. The medium is the message.

Many Websites here in America already do a considerable amount of business outside the United States. With the purchase of two European competitors, Amazon.com has become the leading online bookseller in the UK and Germany. Sales outside the United States currently account for 22 percent of Amazon's sales.

This is a drop in the bucket. The potential is much, much greater. What the postal service did for the Sears, Roebuck catalog, the Internet will do for the American business community. Or, for that matter, any business operating in any country anywhere in the world. The Internet turns the world into one giant shopping mall.

But like in any shopping mall, you can't win with just a better product or service. You need a better brand.

The long-term winners on the Internet will be those brands that can transcend borders. This is another knock on generic names.

What does Furniture.com mean in South America? It certainly doesn't mean *muebles*, the Spanish word for furniture. Or *mobiliário*, the Portuguese word for the same thing.

Amazon.com means *books* in virtually every country of the world. But Books.com means *books* only in the 6 percent of the world where English is the native language.

As the world moves toward a global marketplace, won't companies need to get rid of their national identities and move toward brands with global identities?

Not necessarily. Every brand, including global brands, needs to come from somewhere. In other words, even a global brand needs a national identity.

- Burger King is a global brand with an American identity.

- Volvo is a global brand with a Swedish identity.

- Rolex is a global brand with a Swiss identity.

Like a person, every brand needs to come from somewhere. No matter where the brand is made, marketed, or sold.

A Nissan made in America by American workers is still a Japanese brand of automobile. A Nike made in Malaysia by Malaysian workers is still an American athletic-shoe brand.

What's more important, the product or the brand? The fact that a product can maintain a national identity when the product in question has never set foot in that country should tell you that the brand is more important.

Global brand builders should keep in mind that national identity is a two-edged sword. It can help or hurt your brand, depending upon the category.

American personal computers (built in Asia or with Asian parts) are powerful brands on the global marketplace. American automobiles, no matter where they are built, are mediocre brands everywhere except in America.

What the global market is telling us is that Americans know how to build computers but don't know how to build cars. Is it true? It doesn't matter. When it comes to building brands, perception is more important than reality.

A BMW made in Spartanburg, South Carolina, by American workers using mostly American-made parts is still considered by customers a "German" automobile.

It's hard enough to change the perception of a company. It's impossible for one company to change the perception of a country. When you launch your Internet brand, you should try to match your product or service with your country's perception.

- If we wanted to set up a clothing site on the Internet, we would probably move to Italy and give the site an Italian name.

- If we wanted to sell wine on the Net, we would move to France.

- If we wanted to sell watches on the Net, we would move to Switzerland.

At least that's the theory. In practice it's different. Knowing something about government regulations for wine in France, we would probably choose Chile or Australia instead.

Don't overlook the less developed countries of the world. These nations represent tremendous opportunities for global brand builders wherever they are located. In the less developed countries, retail margins are often higher, fewer products are available, and even fewer products are on display.

For people in some of these countries, many Internet sites will look like the Sears, Roebuck catalog at Wal-Mart prices.

Is it unfair to take advantage of people in developing nations? If offering a better selection of better products at lower prices is unfair, then we don't know the meaning of the word.

Shipping the products (or perhaps we should say "flying" the products) isn't going to be the problem you might think it is. The postal service will airmail a copy of the book you are reading to an address in Europe for less than $10, which is about the retail margin of this book in a domestic bookstore.

And costs are bound to come down dramatically as globalism catches fire and demand for air shipments soars.

One real barrier to globalism is red tape—taxes, duties, customs forms, and paperwork in general. These are the things that are going to clog up the system and slow it down. But you can't stop progress. In time, the paper barriers will come down, too.

Another barrier to globalism is language. The first decision a global brand builder must make is the language question. Do you use English, or do you translate your site into various different languages? Do you set up totally different sites for different countries? Yahoo! launched Yahoo! en Español in 1998 and Yahoo! Brazil in 1999. Today Yahoo! has twenty-three different country sites.

The translation problem can be daunting. How many different languages and/or countries sites should you develop? There are literally thousands of languages in use by the 6 billion people in the world. If you count only the languages used by a significant number of people (say a million or more), there are still 220 different languages. To be a truly global brand, you would need Websites in a substantial percentage of those 220 languages.

Complicating this decision is the long-term trend toward English as the second language of the world. In many countries, English is already the language of business.

(The Scandinavian region of a European company, for example, will inevitably hold its meetings in English. Representatives from Norway, Sweden, Finland, and Denmark may not understand one another when they speak their native languages, but they all know English.)

In the long term you are likely to find successful examples of both single-language and multiple-language sites. Either strategy can work. It all depends upon the type of product or the type of service offered.

For high-tech products and services or for brands appealing to the high-end segment of the market, the single-

Tokyo Tsushin Kogyo?

What do you do if your corporate name is Tokyo Tsushin Kogyo? (It's a name that might work in Japan, but not in the rest of the world.) You change it to Sony. Which is what Tokyo Tsushin Kogyu did in 1958.

Montana has become a very successful Mexican cigarette brand by being the opposite of Marlboro. Instead of using visuals of cowboys on horses, Montana uses visuals of hip people on motorcycles.

language strategy might be best. Cisco.com is an example.

For low-tech products and services or for brands appealing to the mainstream market, a multiple-language strategy might be best. Yahoo! en Español is an example.

(While the thinking at Yahoo! is sound, one part of its strategy is flawed. The line extension name creates the impression that Yahoo! en Español is not an authentic brand. Rather, it's a gringo brand in disguise.)

Keep in mind, however, a basic tenet of marketing: There is never only one way to do anything. Most people prefer brands, but there is still a market for private labels. Most people prefer specialty stores, but there still is a market for department stores. Most people prefer caffeinated cola, regular beer, and coffee, but there is still a market for decaffeinated cola, light beer, and tea.

Whichever language decision you make, you can be sure there will be at least one competitor going in the opposite direction. So be it. You can't appeal to everyone. There is never only one way to do anything.

If you must err, however, err on the side of an English-only site. It will seem more upscale and chic. Time will also be on your side. Every day more than ten thousand people in non-English-speaking countries learn to speak the English language. Furthermore, English is the language of more than 80 percent of the information stored on computers.

There is also a worldwide trend toward the use of English-sounding brand names, even when those brands are sold primarily in non-English-speaking countries.

- *Hollywood* is a brand name for a Brazilian cigarette and also for a French chewing gum.

- *Montana* is a brand name for a Mexican cigarette.

- *Red Bull* is a brand name for an Austrian energy drink that has become a worldwide brand.

- *Boxman* is a brand name for a Swedish online music company.

- *StarMedia* is a brand name for a Spanish- and Portuguese-language Web portal.

Take a walk down the main shopping street of almost any major city in the world. A substantial number of locally owned stores selling locally made goods mostly to local people will have English names.

In Copenhagen, for example, we noticed that about half the stores on the main shopping street use English names. Some of these are franchise operations like McDonald's, Subway, and Athlete's Foot. But most are locally owned stores with names like Inspiration, Planet Football, and London House.

In a Tel Aviv mall, we noticed five stores in a row with the following names: Gold Shop, Happy Tie, Happytime, Royalty, and Make Up Forever.

The trend to English names will obviously benefit all U.S. brands. Before you decide to go with a multiple-language approach, ask yourself whether this trend will make a single-language (English) approach your best overall choice for the future.

Some people think that globalism will be more of a cultural problem than a language problem. That you have to adapt your product or service to the cultures of the countries you are going to sell in. We disagree.

How did Coca-Cola, McDonald's, Levi Strauss, and Subway adapt their brands to local cultural standards? They didn't, and they greatly benefited because they didn't.

The medium is the message. And the message is the homogenization of cultures around the world. That's what globalism is all about. That's neither good nor bad. That's a fact.

When StarMedia was trying to raise capital to launch the first global Internet portal in Spanish and Portuguese, the company got the usual arguments.

Everywhere you go in the world today you see local stores using English names. Jackpot is a women's clothing store in Copenhagen.

This McDonald's in Copenhagen has basically the same menu as a McDonald's in Cleveland. McDonald's became a global brand with only minor changes in its menu. Today the company does more than 60 percent of its business outside the United States.

"Latinos like to have personal contact with each other. Nobody's going to chat online. People want to talk on the phone. Latin Americans are so different from each other, no Argentine will ever want to talk to somebody from Peru."

StarMedia, of course, became a roaring success. Latinos did learn to chat online. People are more alike than different, even though the culture crowd likes to pretend otherwise.

Globalism has benefited from a number of technological developments, notably the jet plane and the facsimile machine. But these developments pale in comparison with the changes the Internet will bring.

So fasten your seat belts and get ready for the ride of your life.

8   THE LAW OF TIME

Just do it. You have to be fast. You have
to be first. You have to be focused.

Haste makes waste, but waste is often the most important
ingredient in a successful Internet launch.

If you want to be successful in business . . . in branding . . . in life . . . you have to get into the mind first. Notice
we said "mind," not "marketplace."

Being first in the marketplace doesn't buy you anything
except a license to try to get in the mind first. If you throw
away that opportunity by being too concerned with getting
all the details right, you'll never get it back. (Perfection in
infinite time is worth nothing.)

What many managers are calling "the first-mover advantage" is a myth. There is no automatic advantage to being
the first mover in a category unless you can make effective
use of the extra time to work your way into the prospect's
mind.

A strategy that many large companies use effectively is
to quickly jump on an idea developed by a smaller company.
With its greater resources, the larger company can often win
"the battle of the mind" and create the perception that it was
first in the marketplace.

If you are the CEO of a smaller company, beware. You
need to move exceptionally fast. Be quick or be dead. Marketplace Darwinism is survival of the fastest.

The first bookstore: Powells.com

Actually, Amazon.com was not the first bookstore on the Internet. Powells.com was. But Powells.com did not take advantage of its early lead to get into the mind of the book-buying public. Being first in the marketplace is useless unless you can also be first in the mind.

First in the mind doesn't mean "early" in the mind either. Too many companies are satisfied with being "one of the first" brands in the category. That's not the same as getting into the mind first and creating the perception that you are the leader.

- Yahoo! was introduced in 1994 as the first search engine on the Internet. Today Yahoo! is the leading search engine and second only to AOL in the rankings of most-visited Websites.

- eBay was introduced in 1995 as the first auction site on the Internet. Today eBay is by far the leading auction site on the Net, with 264 million items listed for sale last year in some eight thousand product categories.

- Amazon.com was introduced in 1995 as the first bookstore on the Internet. Currently the company sells almost $2 billion dollars' worth of books a year, many times that of its nearest competitor, Barnesandnoble.com. Jeff Bezos, Amazon.com's founder, was named *Time* magazine's person of the year for 1999.

- Bluemountain.com was introduced in 1996 as the first electronic greeting-card site. Currently the site receives 10 million unique visitors a month, more than all its competitors combined. The site was sold for $780 million to Excite @ Home, who recently resold it to American Greetings.

- Priceline.com was introduced in 1998 as the first company to sell airline tickets on the Internet with a "name-your-own-price" bidding system. Today Priceline.com is far and away the leading site on the Web for discount airline tickets and hotel rooms. Every seven seconds, someone names their own price at Priceline.com.

Five companies, five brands, five Internet "firsts." And five market leaders whose brands dominate their categories.

Were Yahoo!, eBay, Amazon.com, Bluemountain.com, and Priceline.com literally first in their categories? Amazon.com was not, and we're not sure about the other four.

What you can be sure about is that the ideas for these sites occurred to many other people at about the same time. History shows that ideas tend to arrive in a variety of minds at approximately the same time.

The automobile was "invented" in Germany at about the same time as entrepreneurs in France, England, Italy, and America were working on many of the same self-propelled concepts.

The airplane was "invented" in America, but many French people thought the airplane was invented in France until they read about the Wright brothers accomplishing the same feat several years earlier.

Would we still think the world is flat if it weren't for Christopher Columbus? Of course not. Somebody else would have discovered America and realized the world was round.

Would we still be communicating with smoke signals if it weren't for Alexander Graham Bell? Of course not. Somebody else would have invented the telephone.

Would we still be using Thermofax copiers if it weren't for Chester Carlson? Of course not. Somebody else would have invented xerography.

There's a big difference between having an idle thought on a Sunday afternoon and having a successful brand on the Internet on Monday morning. Ideas (and those idle thoughts that initiate them) are a dime a dozen. It takes hard work and, even more important, a sense of urgency to put an idea to work on the Net.

You can't dawdle. By this we mean endless testing, focus groups, market surveys. This is a particular problem for an Internet brand.

Why were most of the successful Internet sites launched by small, venture-capital-backed companies rather than *For-*

In 1885, Karl Benz demonstrated a three-wheeled self-propelled vehicle. The following year Gottlieb Daimler demonstrated a four-wheeler. Later they merged to form Daimler-Benz, the world's first automobile company.

Financial services

Today the big companies are coming into the Internet arena with massive self-confidence and massive budgets. GE Financial Services is a typical example. There are three reasons why GEfs.com won't make it:

1. Wrong name
2. Wrong strategy (lack of focus)
3. Too late

tune 500 firms? A big company hates to do anything without first amassing a mound of market research.

The Internet is moving too fast to be measured. It's a new industry. Knowledge is scarce. Few people know what they want, what they would use, what they would be willing to pay for . . . until they are given a real-world choice.

Big companies often fail to exploit new opportunities because they are "perfectionists." They won't release a new product, a new service, or an Internet site "until we get it right."

Getting it right makes no sense from a branding point of view. Anything worth doing is worth doing in a half-assed way. Anything not worth doing is not worth doing in a perfect way.

Take Yahoo!, the most valuable brand on the Internet. Yahoo! is basically a search engine. It will find whatever you want to find on the Internet.

Yahoo! is the top search engine in almost every major country in the world. It generates 40 percent of all search referrals worldwide.

Did Yahoo! develop its own search-engine technology? No. In order to move rapidly, it outsourced its search-engine technology, first from Open Source, then from AltaVista, before finally settling on Inktomi.

The leading search engine didn't develop its own search-engine technology? Does that surprise you? It shouldn't. You don't win by being better. You win by being first. Yahoo! succeeded because they "rushed the net."

One of the abiding myths of American business is that you win by being better. Management commits billions of dollars in their search for better products or services to market. They "benchmark" their existing products and services against their major competitors. No new product or service gets launched unless it has a significant, tangible advantage.

Result: Nine out of ten new products fail. Why? Not, in our opinion, because of a quality deficiency. It's because of a timing deficiency. They didn't get that new product or service out in the marketplace fast enough.

Big companies often lack a sense of urgency when it comes to introducing new products or new ideas. Sometimes you can detect that in their public statements. "Maybe we are relatively late," said Rupert Murdoch, CEO of News Corp., when he recently announced the company's first Internet investment, "but only by a year or two."

Only by a year or two? In less than two years, Priceline.com went from nothing to market leadership of a new category on the Internet.

Carpe diem. Where would Microsoft be today if Bill Gates hadn't dropped out of Harvard in his freshman year to go to Albuquerque, New Mexico, to develop an operating system for the world's first personal computer?

Carpe diem. Where would Dell Computer be today if Michael Dell hadn't dropped out of the University of Texas in his sophomore year to start a company selling computers directly to businesses.

Carpe diem. Today is the best day of your life to launch an Internet company based on a new idea or concept. One that nobody else is using.

Have you ever heard of NorthernLight.com? You're not alone. More than 99 percent of Web users are not familiar with the site.

Northern Light Technology LLC was the largest search engine on the Internet, in the sense that it indexed some 330 million Web pages. That's far more than Yahoo!, Excite, Lycos, or Infoseek. Plus Northern Light compiled the contents of some six thousand full-text sources such as business magazines, trade journals, medical publications, investment databases, and news wires.

The problem wasn't the site. The problem was the timing. Northern Light didn't get turned on until three years after the Yahoo! launch. That's much too late. Not only was Yahoo! gathering momentum, but the new search site also

You missed it. When this book was first published, venture capital was easy to come by. Today it's exceedingly difficult to raise funds for an Internet venture. It's not impossible, however. All you need is patience, hard work, and a good idea. Especially a good idea.

had to compete with AltaVista, Excite, Infoseek, and Lycos.

The problem wasn't the money. Northern Light was financed with $50 million in venture capital, far more than Yahoo! had to work with.

It's bad enough to start in second place. It's worse to start at the back of the pack. In many situations it's almost hopeless.

So what do you do if you're late? Too many managers put on their Avis hats and say "We have to try harder." Not good enough. (Remember the Law of Singularity.)

Paradoxically, it's never too late. But you can't launch in the year 2003 a great idea, circa 1995. If you get into the game late, you have to narrow your focus. Michael Dell was late, very late, into personal computers. So he decided to focus on selling personal computers by telephone. A good strategy. Today Dell Computer is the world's largest manufacturer of personal computers.

Michael Dell didn't make the same mistake when the Internet arrived. His company was the first to sell personal computers on the Web. Also a good strategy.

Nor is it ever enough just to move rapidly without a basically good idea. Time Warner was one of the first companies to set up an Internet site. Hence the name, Pathfinder.

But what's a Pathfinder? At first the site was nothing more than a collection of information pulled from various Time Warner magazines: *Time, People, Fortune, Money, Entertainment Weekly,* and others. After the purchase of Turner Broadcasting System, the company added CNN, CNNsi and CNNfn to the site. They even managed to sell American Express on listing *Travel & Leisure* magazine on the site as well as *Asia Week,* a Hong Kong publication, now deceased.

After investing a reported $75 million in the site, Time Warner recently shut it down. What's a Pathfinder? The only meaning the name had was that it was a site for Time Warner publications. But few people care who publishes a magazine (unless John F. Kennedy Jr. is involved, and as soon as he was gone, *George* magazine was gone, too). They only care about the magazine itself.

Nobody reads *Fortune* because Time Warner publishes it. They read *Fortune* in spite of the fact that Time Warner publishes it. The name of the company that publishes the magazine is irrelevant to the average reader. *Fortune* is the brand, not Time Warner.

After Time Warner gave up on Pathfinder, the company retreated to individual sites for each of its major publications. Also not a good strategy. (Line-extension sites of magazine brands might be good for selling a few subscriptions, but they are not the way to build a powerful presence on the Web.)

Time Warner bills itself as the "world's foremost media company." How could two yahoos from Stanford beat the world's foremost media company?

Easy. All you need to do is to get your strategy right and your timing right. Both are required. One without the other won't work.

P.S.: You probably noticed that it was AOL that took over Time Warner and not vice versa.

George magazine died a quick death in 2001. It's hard to keep a celebrity magazine alive in the absence of the celebrity.

9   THE LAW OF VANITY

The biggest mistake of all is believing
you can do anything.

Success in business doesn't just show up on the bottom line of the profit-and-loss column; it also goes to the top. Success in business inflates the egos of top management.

Supremely successful companies believe they can do anything. They can launch any product into any market. They can make any merger work. It's just a question of having the willpower and the resources to throw into the task. What is it that we want to do? is the question that management usually asks itself.

History hasn't been kind to this type of thinking. Overconfident management has been responsible for most of the marketing disasters of the past decades.

- General Electric couldn't crack the mainframe computer market in spite of its reputation for brilliant management.

- Sears, Roebuck's "socks and stocks" strategy of selling brokerage accounts, insurance, and real estate in its retail stores went nowhere.

- Xerox couldn't duplicate its copier success in computers.

- IBM, on the other hand, couldn't extend its computer success to copiers.

- Kodak lost its focus when it tried to get into instant photography.

- Polaroid, on the other hand, fared no better in conventional 35mm film.

Xerox bought Scientific Data Systems for nearly a billion dollars' worth of stock, changed the name to Xerox Data Systems, and then launched the brand with an advertisement that read, "This Xerox machine can't make a copy." Any Xerox machine that can't make a copy is in deep trouble.

Get the picture? As soon as a company is successful in one area, it tries to move into another. Generally with little or no success.

The problem is usually not the new product or service being offered. Xerox may well have had the best computer product on the market. The problem is in the mind of the prospect. "What does a copier company know about computers?"

In other words, the problem is not a product problem, it's a perception problem. The most difficult problem in business today is trying to change a perception that exists in the mind of a customer or prospect. Once a perception is strongly held in the mind, it can almost never be changed. (Anybody who has ever been married knows the difficulty of changing a perception in another person's mind.)

What's a Cadillac? In the mind of the car buyer, it's a "big car." But the market started shifting to smaller cars. So naturally Cadillac tried to sell a small Cadillac called the Catera, with very little success. On the other hand, the Cadillac Escalade, a big SUV, looks like it is going to be an enormous success.

What's a Volkswagen? In the mind of the car buyer, it's a "small car." But its customers now have families. So naturally Volkswagen tried to sell a larger Volkswagen called the Passat, with very little success.

Cadillac couldn't sell small Cadillacs. And Volkswagen couldn't sell big Volkswagens.

Once you stand for something in the prospect's mind, it's hard to change what you stand for. Volkswagen stands for small. Cadillac stands for big. Can you change these percep-

The Volkswagen brand stands for "small, ugly, and reliable." When the company introduced a car (the New Beetle) that matched those perceptions, it was instantly successful. Instead of trying to change minds, companies should try to exploit existing perceptions.

tions? (And, furthermore, why would you want to?)

Unlikely. Yet they keep trying. Before the Catera launch, Cadillac tried selling the Cimarron, another smaller Cadillac. Predictably the Cimarron also never got out of the garage.

The folks at Lincoln ought to be laughing at Cadillac's predicament, but they're not. They too are busy introducing the new small Lincoln (LS for Lincoln Small, of course).

Meanwhile the three-and-a-half-ton Lincoln Navigator is doing great. When a new product matches the perceptions that already exist in the mind, the new product can be exceedingly successful.

When Volkswagen brought back the Beetle, their original small car, sales exploded. As you might expect, the success of the New Beetle also went to their heads. There's no reason we can't sell $60,000 cars with the Volkswagen name on them, said one VW executive recently. Yes, there is. People won't buy them.

Will the online world be any different than the off-line world? We think not. To be successful on the Internet you still have to do business with human minds. Once you stand for something in a mind, it's hard to change the perception of what you stand for.

Amazon.com was the first Internet site to sell books and music CDs. The site is a roaring success, with current sales of $3.1 billion annually (albeit with losses in the past year of $567 million).

When you are named *Time* magazine's "Person of the Year" at age thirty-five, as Jeff Bezos was, you can be forgiven for thinking you can do anything. Amazon.com's expansion into a bewildering variety of products and services makes no sense except as a reflection of management's ego.

So what is Amazon.com doing next? You know what they're doing next. They're in the process of turning themselves into a "destination site" where customers can find anything they could possibly want.

- DVDs and videotapes

- Electronics and software

- Toys and video games

- Home improvement products

- A gift-registry system

- E-cards

- Auctions, including a joint venture with Sotheby's (Amazon spent $45 million for a 1.7 percent stake in Sotheby's)

- zShops, where thousands of small merchants can do business under the Amazon.com banner

- Credit cards in a cobranded arrangement with NextCard Inc. (Amazon.com also spent $22.5 million for a warrant that lets it acquire 9.9 percent of the credit-card company)

- Automobiles in a deal with CarsDirect.com

Wow! What a list. But, hey, if you're "person of the year," you ought to be able to do all of these things.

Amazon.com used to use the theme "Earth's Biggest Bookstore." No longer. They've changed it. The new theme is "Earth's Biggest Selection."

Person of the year Jeff Bezos, CEO of Amazon.com, says, "It's very natural for a customer to wonder, can you really be the best place to buy music, books, and electronics? In the physical world, the answer is almost always no. But on the Internet all the physical constraints go away." (A sign of the times: The company recently registered "Amazoneverywhere.net as a Website name.)

All the physical constraints may go away on the Internet, but what about the mental constraints? What about the mind of the prospect? What's an Amazon.com?

If Xerox is copiers, IBM is computers, Cadillac is big cars, and Volkswagen is small cars, then Amazon.com is an Internet bookstore.

If Amazon.com is an Internet bookstore, then how come the site has also been able to successfully sell music CDs?

What's an Amazon?

In order to finance its expansion into other areas, Amazon.com tried to raise book prices. This is a lose-lose strategy. It makes the company vulnerable to lower-priced book competitors while at the same time it pursues other markets it can't possibly conquer.

Blockbuster means "movie rentals." So what's a Blockbuster Music store? Your first impression is that Blockbuster Music must be a store that rents music CDs. But that doesn't make sense. Who would want to rent a music CD? Confusion was one of the factors in the failure of the Blockbuster Music concept.

And if they can successfully sell music CDs, why can't they also sell toys and electronics?

Look around your community at big bookstores like Borders or Waldenbooks. Do they sell toys and electronics? No. But they do sell music CDs. Ergo: The customer associates music CDs with bookstores.

"There's no reason for Amazon not to sell other merchandise," said Bill Gates recently. Yes, there is. It's called "perception," and it's a critical attribute of the human mind. Amazon.com means Internet bookstore. Not auctions, gifts, home-improvement products, toys, video games, electronics, software, DVDs, or videotapes.

You see Amazon.com thinking all over the physical world. Blockbuster means video rentals. "There's no reason for Blockbuster Video not to sell other merchandise," someone at corporate headquarters probably muttered to themselves a number of years ago. So Blockbuster Music was born.

After years of losses, the company finally faced the music and spun off the division in 1999. The new name: Wherehouse Music.

"You'll see more Amazon-like cases in which a company that is strong in one online area expands its product offerings," adds Bill Gates. Sure, you will. Line extension is very popular in corporate America, almost as popular as stock options and corporate jets. Both feed the corporate ego.

What is terribly confusing is the fact that line extension can work . . . in the short term. But almost never in the long term.

This is especially true if you are the first in a new category. When you are the first, when you dominate a new category, you can be successful in the short term taking the line-extension route. You may pay the price later, but you can easily fool yourself into thinking that you are going in the right direction when you broaden your approach.

Take Yahoo!, for example. Incredibly the company's mission statement is "to be all things to all people" (a phrase reportedly repeated as a mantra by many Yahoo! executives).

Starting as a search engine on the Internet, Yahoo! has now expanded its Website to include the following features: auctions, calendars, chat rooms, classifieds, e-mail, games, maps, news, pager services, people searches, personals, radio, shopping, sports, stock quotes, weather reports, and yellow pages.

To further its goal of being all things to all people, Yahoo! has also spent a small fortune on a raft of acquisitions.

- $5 billion for Broadcast.com, a service that delivers audio and video over the Internet

- $3.7 billion for GeoCities, a home-page service

- $130 million for Encompass, a technology company that makes software to more easily link consumers to Internet services

- $80 million for Online Anywhere, a technology that allows the company to deliver information and services to a wide variety of non-PC devices

Is Yahoo! successful? (Silly question, the company is worth $11 billion on the stock market.)

Sure, Yahoo! is successful, but the brand had the enormous advantage of being the first search engine on the Internet. As a result, Yahoo! received an inordinate amount of publicity.

Yahoo! became a celebrity brand. In one seventeen-month period, in six thousand different news media, Yahoo! received an astounding forty-five thousand citations, far greater than any other Internet site.

Nothing succeeds like excess. With enough favorable media mentions, Mussolini Merlot might become a popular brand of Italian wine.

But nothing lasts forever. The media will move on to the next hot Internet brand, leaving Yahoo! in the uncomfortable position of having to spend its own money to communicate its identity.

> **Yahoo's mission:
> "To be all things
> to all people."**

Yahoo!'s mission statement, "To be all things to all people," a phrase repeated as a mantra by Yahoo! executives, is bound to get the company in trouble. Recently CEO Tim Koogle was replaced by the Yahoo! board, and Terry Semel from Warner Bros. was brought in to take his place.

Apple Computer suffers from a lack of focus. It's the only major personal computer company that tries to market both hardware and software, including its own operating system. Hardware leader Dell Computer doesn't market its own software, and software leader Microsoft doesn't market its own computers.

What's a Yahoo!? Not an easy question to answer when you are "all things to all people."

Leaders tend to self-destruct when they blow themselves up. When you try to be everything, you end up being nothing.

Apple started as a personal computer hardware company, then moved into software, operating systems, and personal digital assistants. Apple lost its way, its CEO, and almost its entire existence until Steve Jobs retook the reins and refocused Apple on its core business, easy-to-use and "insanely great" personal computers.

But everybody wants to grow, and you can't blame them. So what should an Internet brand like Amazon.com do? There are five fundamental branding strategies for a leader in any category.

1. KEEP YOUR BRAND FOCUSED.

There are more than 22 million dotcom sites registered on the Internet, and you want your site to stand for more than one thing? Amazon.com should stay focused on books and music CDs. After all, the site accounts for just 8 percent of the $25 billion book market in the United States.

2. INCREASE YOUR SHARE OF THE MARKET.

The time to think about getting into another business is after you dominate the business you're already in. Until Amazon.com has at least 25 percent of the book market, it should stick to its knitting. Its short-term strategy should focus on finding ways to increase its 8 percent market share.

3. EXPAND YOUR MARKET.

Leaders should figure out how to expand their market, knowing that many of the benefits of a larger market will flow to them. What about book clubs, chat rooms with authors, and other book-building activities, including Amazon-sponsored seminars by famous authors?

4. GO GLOBAL.

Sure, the Internet is a worldwide information and communications network already, but Amazon.com's share of the book market outside the United States is minuscule. (Currently the company sells only 22 percent of its books overseas.)

Amazon.com should make a major effort to reach customers in the rest of the world. As English becomes the business language of the world, the market for books in English should skyrocket.

Why stop at English? Amazon.com should take its Internet expertise into all the major languages of the world.

Thinking often stops at the border. The most successful companies today treat the world as their oyster.

5. DOMINATE THE CATEGORY.

For a leading brand, a 25 percent market share should be a conservative goal. With a quarter of the U.S. book market, Amazon.com would rack up sales of $6.3 billion, enough to put the company on the *Fortune* 500 list, ahead of such companies as Southwest Airlines, Avon Products, Campbell Soup, Sherwin-Williams, Ryder Systems, Nordstrom, Owens Corning, Black & Decker, and Hershey Foods.

Nothing works in branding as well as market domination. Coca-Cola in cola, Hertz in car rentals, Budweiser in beer, Goodyear in tires, Microsoft in personal computer operating systems, Intel in microprocessors, Cisco in networking equipment, Oracle in database software, Intuit in personal finance software.

Microsoft

Power in marketing is directly related to market domination. Microsoft is a powerful brand not because the company produces better software (although it might) but because the company has 95 percent of the personal computer operating systems market and 92 percent of the office suite market.

Amazon.com has a once-in-a-lifetime opportunity to dominate the book business on a worldwide scale. Why throw away this opportunity in order to chase a dozen other markets, none of which they are likely to dominate?

Still, when the vanity bug bites you, it's hard to resist. "We can get into these other markets. We have the products, we have the people, we have the systems, we have the momentum, and we have the esprit de corps. Why not?"

Why not? You may have everything going for you, including the products, the people, and the systems, but you lack one thing. You lack the perception.

The issue in branding, Internet or otherwise, always boils down to the same thing: product versus perception.

Many managers believe it's only necessary to deliver a better product or service to win. But brands like Coca-Cola, Hertz, Budweiser, and Goodyear are strong not because they have the best product or service (although they might have) but because they are market leaders that dominate their categories.

Which scenario seems more likely, A or B?

Scenario A: The company creates a better product or service and consequently achieves market leadership.

Scenario B: The company achieves market leadership (usually by being first in a new category) and then subsequently achieves the perception of having the better product or service.

Logic suggests Scenario A, but history is overwhelmingly on the side of Scenario B. Leadership first, perception second.

AltaVista bills itself as "the most powerful and useful guide to the Net." We have no reason to doubt their claim. But is this enough to enable AltaVista to wrestle the portal leadership away from Yahoo!? Not in our opinion.

Leadership first, perception second. To try to reverse this sequence is almost impossible.

What if you do everything right? What if you are the first in a new category and subsequently go on to dominate that category domestically? Then you should try to expand the market in the U.S. at the same time that you take your brand to the global market.

Coca-Cola did all of these things. But what's next? Are there no second acts in branding history?

Most assuredly there are. A company can do two things at once (keep a narrow focus and expand its business) by the simple strategy of launching a second, or even a third and fourth, brand.

One effective strategy is to use your leadership position to "characterize your competition." In its advertising, Hertz describes all the extra services it offers and then characterizes its competitors as "not exactly Hertz."

- Coca-Cola owns Coca-Cola, the leading cola, and Sprite, the leading lemon-lime soda.

- Anheuser-Busch owns Budweiser, the leading regular beer; Michelob, the leading premium beer; and Busch, the leading low-price beer.

- Darden Restaurants owns Olive Garden, the leading Italian restaurant chain, and Red Lobster, the leading seafood restaurant chain. (Darden is the world's largest casual dining company.)

- Toyota also owns Lexus.

- Black & Decker also owns DeWalt.

- Levi Strauss owns both Levi's and Dockers.

- The Gap also owns Banana Republic and Old Navy.

America Online is using the same multiple-brand strategy on the Internet. AOL is its premium brand for which subscribers pay $23.90 a month. The service includes nineteen separate topic channels, fifteen thousand chat rooms, and ICQ, a popular instant messaging capability. CompuServe is the company's value brand. It's a good deal. For $19.95 a month, CompuServe gives you everything AOL gives you except for the AOL e-mail address.

Instead of launching second brands, however, most companies take the vanity route instead. "What's wrong with our name? We're famous. Why do we need a second brand? We can use our own name on that line extension."

Some companies that practice line extension seem to be successful, at least in the short term. Microsoft is a good example.

After dominating the personal computer operating system business, Microsoft has gone into a raft of different businesses, all under the Microsoft name. "If Microsoft can do it, why can't we?" is a constant refrain of our consulting clients.

Our answer: You're not Microsoft. When you have 95 percent of a market, when you are worth $332 billion on the stock market, you are extremely powerful. You can do almost anything and still appear to be successful.

Leadership changes the rules of the game. Try telling your spouse, "If Bill Clinton can do it, why can't I?"

Most CEOs are not Bill Clinton either. They are not the former leader of the most powerful country in the world. They have to follow ordinary rules.

Leaders, especially dominant leaders like Microsoft, can break all the laws and still stay on top . . . for now.

Look again at Yahoo!, a company that is following the Microsoft game plan. Former CEO Timothy Koogle said: "In online commerce and shopping you can expect to see us extend aggressively by broadening and deepening the range of consumer buying, transaction, and fulfillment services we provide across all major categories." (Maybe this is one reason that Koogle is gone.)

Don't be too critical of Yahoo!'s behavior. You only live once. Being young and rich and foolish is a lot more fun than being old and wise.

Many sites are going in the same direction, but without

Yahoo!'s powerful brand-name recognition. They include Buy.com, Shopping.com, Shopnow.com, and a host of other copycat sites. "Anything you want to buy, we can get it for you at a discount."

What does a site like BuyItNow.com sell? Jewelry, consumer electronics, toys, kitchen equipment, home decorating products, sporting goods, tools, pet supplies, garden supplies, gifts, luxury items. "You name it, we've got it."(It should come as no surprise that BuyItNow.com is no longer with us.)

Snap.com goes one step further. Not only can you buy everything by visiting the Snap site, but you can buy it from any store. "Any product. Any store. Any time. Snap shopping" is the theme. Vanity is working overtime at Snap.com.

As Internet fever cools down, as the Internet becomes just one of the places you can go to buy things, those generic sites that sell everything to everybody are unlikely to be with us. Yahoo!, on the other hand, is in no danger because it has a powerful, dominant position in the portal category. As does Amazon.com in the books and music category.

A question remains for leader brands like Yahoo! and Amazon.com. Would these companies have been better off with a multiple-brand strategy rather than a line-extension strategy?

We think so. But it is getting harder and harder to find leaders that want to introduce second brands.

Their vanity leads them astray.

> **Any product. Any store. Any time.**
>
> The ultimate in vanity was Snap.com's offer to sell you any product from any store at any time of the day or night. Snap.com was folded into NBCi.com, which was also eventually shut down.

10   THE LAW OF DIVERGENCE

Everyone talks about convergence, while
just the opposite is happening.

Whenever a new medium hits town, the cry goes up, "Convergence, convergence. What is this new medium going to converge with?"

When television hit town, there were stories everywhere about the convergence of TV with magazines and newspapers. You weren't going to get your magazines in the mail anymore. When you wanted an issue, you would hit the button on your TV set and the issue would be printed out in your living room. (We don't make these things up. We just report the facts.)

When the Internet arrived, the same type of stories appeared. Now you can surf the Net while you watch TV. (Microsoft's WebTV is the leading supplier of this service.)

Many companies have tried to combine a television set with a personal computer, with a notable lack of success—Apple, Gateway, and others.

Convergence has become an obsession at Microsoft. "Has William H. Gates become the Captain Ahab of the information age?" asked the *New York Times* recently. "Mr. Gates' white whale remains an elusive digital set-top cable box that his company, the Microsoft Corporation, is hoping will re-create the personal computer industry by blending the PC, the Internet and the television set into a leviathan living-room entertainment and information machine."

The PC, the Internet, and the television set will combine? It will never happen. Technologies don't converge. They diverge.

Many Internet branders are falling into the convergence trap. They look for ways to blend the real world with the Internet world. Their ingenuity knows no bounds.

- Newspapers and magazines on the Internet

- Radio and television on the Internet

- Internet service on your telephone or from your PalmPilot

- Facsimile and telephone service from your computer or television set

The media have been fanning the convergence fire for a long time. According to a 1993 article in the *Wall Street Journal*:

Shock is a common feeling these days among leaders of five of the world's biggest industries: computing, communications, consumer electronics, entertainment and publishing. Under a common technological lash— the increasing ability to cheaply convey huge chunks of video, sound, graphics and text in digital form—they are transforming and converging.

The *New York Times* put it this way the same year:

Digital convergence is not a futuristic prospect or a choice to be made among other choices; it is an onrushing train. The digitalization of all forms of information (including the transmission of sensations) has proven itself to be accurate, economical, ecologically wise, universally applicable, easy to use, and fast as light.

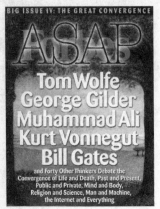

Forbes ASAP published a special issue entitled "The Great Convergence" featuring forty-four great thinkers, including Tom Wolfe, George Gilder, Muhammad Ali, Kurt Vonnegut, and Bill Gates. The editorial introduction to the issue contained these breathless words: "Great ideas have changed us many times before. We divide much of human history by the dates they emerged: fire, the domestication of animals, farming and trade, democracy, empires, the divine right of kings, perspective, Newtonian mechanics, liberty, mass production, the nation-state, evolution and relativity, fission, abstraction, digitization, equality. The emerging idea of our time is convergence. It is the governing metaphor of the turn of the millennium."

Fortune was just as enthusiastic in 1993:

Convergence will be the buzzword for the rest of the decade. This isn't just about cable and telephone hopping into bed together. It's about the cultures and corporations of major industries—telecommunications (including the long-distance companies), cable, computers, entertainment, consumer electronics, publishing, and even retailing—combining into one mega-industry that will provide information, entertainment, goods, and services to your home and office.

The media are putting their money where their mouths are. In Europe, the *Wall Street Journal* publishes a monthly magazine insert called "Convergence." *Business Week* runs an annual conference entitled "The Global Convergence Summit."

With the media running off at the mouth about the convergence concept, is it any wonder that many corporations were all too eager to jump on the convergence bandwagon?

When asked by *Fortune* magazine what unique opportunities Compaq was looking at, the new CEO, Michael Capellas, said: "You'll start to see devices converge. Who in the world doesn't want to have their PalmPilot, their telephone, and their CD player all wrapped into one so they don't have to carry three things on their belt?"

It will never happen. Technologies don't converge. They diverge. Yet the hype marches on.

According to famous futurist Faith Popcorn, "Someday in the near future I'll be watching *Ally McBeal*. I like the outfit she's wearing. So I put my hand on the TV screen and she'll interrupt the program and say, 'Faith, do you like what I'm wearing?' 'Yeah,' I'll say. 'I like your suit.' And she'll say, 'Here are the colors it comes in.' I'll tell Ally that I'll take just navy or black, maybe both. And she'll say, 'No you won't, Faith. You've already got too many navy and black outfits in

your closet right now. I think you should try red this time.'
And I'll say okay, and the next day the red suit is delivered,
in my size, to my home."

When asked how soon this would happen, the famous
futurist replied, "Within the next five years."

Don't hold your breath. Ally McBeal will be lucky if her
TV show is still on in five years, never mind her personal
shopping advice service.

While television sets and telephones are supposedly
becoming computers, computers are supposedly becoming
appliances that can receive television and radio programming as well as telephone calls.

Broadcast.com, for example, offers live broadcasts of
more than thirty television stations and 370 radio stations.
All available on your computer through the magic of the
Internet. Meanwhile, rival Real Networks has put together
more than 1,100 live stations on their lineup. Competitor
InterVU has put together a network focused on business
services.

Will people watch television programming on their computers? Sure, some people will, but most television viewing
is likely to continue to be done on TV sets.

The truth is, technologies diverge. They don't converge.
A quick look at history validates the division theory.

- Radio used to be just radio. Today we have AM radio
  and FM radio. We also have portable radios, car radios,
  headset radios, clock radios, cable radio, and satellite
  radio. Radio didn't combine with another medium. It
  diverged.

- Television used to be just television. Today we have
  broadcast TV, cable TV, satellite TV, pay-per-view TV.
  Television didn't combine with another medium. It
  diverged.

We were talking about
divergence at a seminar in
Helsinki when a man in
the back row interrupted
our presentation by pulling
out his Nokia 9110
Communicator and shouting,
"What are you talking about?
Convergence is happening,
I have it right in my hand."
We stopped the meeting,
walked to the back of the
room, and compared our tiny
Nokia cell phone with his
9110 Communicator. "Look,"
we said, "ours is the size and
weight of a cigarette package
and yours is the size and
weight of a brick. Who wants
to carry a brick to make a
phone call?"

- The telephone used to be just the telephone. Today we have regular telephones, cordless telephones, car phones, cell phones, and satellite phones. Also analog and digital phones. The telephone didn't combine with another communications technology. It diverged.

- The computer used to be just a computer. Today we have mainframe computers, midrange computers, minicomputers, network computers, personal computers, notebook computers, and handheld computers. The computer didn't combine with another technology. It diverged.

People often confuse what's possible with what's practical. After Neil Armstrong and Buzz Aldrin walked on the moon in 1969, the media were filled with stories about future colonists in space. Where they would live. What they would eat. How they would work.

(The moon is a great place to visit, but how many people would want to live there?)

What's possible won't happen just because it's possible. It also has to be practical. A computer and TV combination would seem like a natural, but Apple, Toshiba, Gateway, and others have launched combination products that failed.

Recently Philips went one step further. In addition to a computer and a television tuner, the Philips DVX8000 features an FM/AM radio and a CD/DVD player. What more could you want?

Simplicity, ease of use, reliability, light weight, protection against early obsolescence, and low cost, for example.

Instead of accessing the Internet from your home television set, it is much more likely that you will someday have an Internet appliance. An electronic machine devoted to Internet connections only, especially for e-mail use.

Actually, there are a number of such products on the market, ranging in price from $100 to $200 plus the service fee. They include the MailStation by Cidco, TelMail by Sharp Elec-

The BlackBerry by Research In Motion was the first wireless e-mail device. It has become very successful, especially among corporate executives.

tronic, the MailBug by Landel Telecom, and the PostBox from VTech Industries. (The BlackBerry is another divergence device that has quite a few enthusiastic users.)

Why are divergence products generally winners and convergence products generally losers? One reason is that convergence products are always a compromise. The Intel microprocessor inside the Philips DVX8000 should be good for three years or so. The home-theater half of the machine should last twenty years.

Before televisions combine with computers, you would think TV sets would combine with videocassette recorders. You can buy combination TV/VCRs, of course, but most people don't. Recently we visited a consumer electronics store that had a wall full of such products.

"How are sales of your combination television/VCRs?" we asked the clerk. "Infinitesimal," he replied.

Nor are many combination washer/dryers sold. Or microwave/stoves. Or telephone/telephone answering machines. Or copier/printer/fax machines.

The one glimmer of hope for the convergence concept is the clock radio. Enthusiasts are fond of citing the clock radio as a brilliant example of the power of convergence thinking. But in some ways, a clock radio is not a dual function device at all. Rather, it's a single-function music alarm clock, a way of getting you out of bed in the morning without the shock of an earth-shattering noise. Not many people use their clock radios as a way to play the radio.

Other than the clock radio, the history of convergence products has been rather dismal. After World War II, the two biggest industries in America were the automotive industry and the airplane industry. Sure enough, pundits thought that the car was going to converge with the plane.

In 1946, Ted Hall introduced his Flying Car, which was received by a wildly enthusiastic public. Roads soon would become obsolete, traffic jams a thing of the past. You could go anywhere, anytime, with complete freedom of movement.

Convergenists are fond of citing the clock-radio as an example of a successful convergence product. But the clock did not really combine with the radio. Most clocks do not have radios, and most radios do not have clocks. Rather, the clock-radio is a unique device that serves a single function.

The 1946 Hall Flying Car looked a little goofy, which may have been one reason it never went into production.

Every major aircraft manufacturer in America hoped to cash in on Hall's invention. The lucky buyer was Convair.

In July of that year, Convair introduced Hall's flight of fancy as the Convair Model 118 ConvAirCar. Company management confidently predicted minimum sales of 160,000 units a year. The price was $1,500 plus an extra charge for the wings, which would also be available for rental at any airport.

In spite of the hype, only two ConvAirCars were ever built. Both are now said to rest in a warehouse in El Cajon, California.

Three years later, Moulton Taylor introduced the Aerocar, a sporty runabout with detachable wings and tail. The Aerocar received a tremendous amount of publicity at the time. The Ford Motor Company considered mass-producing it. But Taylor's Aerocar met with the same predictable fate as Hall's Flying Car.

The 1949 Taylor Aerocar was a step forward in flying-car design, but it still didn't get produced in quantity.

It's divergence that almost always triumphs, not convergence. Today we have many types of airplanes (jet planes, prop planes, helicopters) and many types of automobiles (sedans, convertibles, station wagons, sport utility vehicles), but almost no flying cars.

Would-be convergenists should also study the combination automobile/boat introduced with great fanfare by Amphicar, a German company. Like all convergence products, the Amphicar performed neither function very well. "Drives like a boat, floats like a car," was the buyers' verdict.

Bad ideas never really die. Paul Moller has spent thirty-five years developing the Skycar, a personal flying machine that is as easy to use as a car. Today, $50 million, forty-three patents, and three wives later, his dream is ready for liftoff.

The 1961 Amphicar was launched with high hopes and a huge promotional budget. Yet, it met the same fate as virtually all convergence products.

Don't laugh. What will look foolish several decades from now is often taken seriously today. As recently as June 24, 1999, the *Wall Street Journal* ran a major article on Moller's sky dream on the front page of its Marketplace section. (Professor Moller has taken seventy-two orders, with a $5,000 deposit, for the Skycar.)

What motivates Moller also motivates Microsoft. The company poured millions of dollars into WebTV, a major effort to turn America's 100 million television-owning households into Internet explorers.

Sure, WebTV is closing in on 1 percent of the market, but does any convergence product have much of a future?

There's a lot of evidence that mixing "interactivity," an Internet attribute, with the "passivity" of the television experience just isn't going to work. Time Warner introduced the Full Service Network, the first digital interactive TV network, in Orlando, Florida, in 1994 and shut it down two years later.

A company called ACTV was founded in 1989 to bring interactive TV to the public. On average the company has lost $7 million a year for the past decade. Finally, ACTV is rolling out its first product in partnership with Fox Sports. For $10 a month, Fox fans will be able to use their remote control to click on to different camera angles, pull up stats, or cut to instant replays at any time during the game.

Will the average couch potato want to put down his Bud Light long enough to change the camera angle? We don't think so. At least not when it's third down and goal to go for the home team.

TV directors get paid big bucks to do that for us. Why would the average viewer want to do it for nothing?

Not only that. Spending the time figuring out the best camera angle will cause the watcher to miss the play. Not to mention the frustrations of the other people in the room who do not have the remote control in their hands.

Technology tends to triumph over logic. "If you build it, they will come." Bill Gates, the manager of the high-technology team, is getting his players involved in convergence in a big way. In addition to his WebTV investment, Gates put $5 billion of Microsoft's money into AT&T to help the company purchase a cable TV operation. In return, AT&T has agreed to license a minimum of five million copies of Microsoft's Windows CE operating system.

The 1991 Moller Skycar had eight engines and was estimated to cost $800,000, which would put it out of reach of most drivers.

Microsoft spent $425 million to buy WebTV and then poured another $500 million into developing the system. Now Microsoft has more or less given up on WebTV and moved on to something called "Ultimate TV." Both systems are bound to fail because they are based on convergence concepts.

The two companies hoped that a General Instrument set-top box, the DTC-5000, would be the entry point for all the digital information flowing into the home. In addition to five hundred channels of interactive cable, the DTC-5000 would also handle telephone service, video on demand, stereo audio, video games, and Internet access.

Recently AT&T backed out of its commitment to Microsoft, leaving 240,000 of those advanced set-top boxes gathering dust in a warehouse.

The Skycar, the Amphicar, the set-top box. Billions of dollars have been wasted chasing the convergence dream. But why do we make such a federal case out of the convergence follies?

Because brands cannot be built with convergence thinking. Unless you can clearly see the fallacy behind the convergence concept, you are unlikely to build a successful Internet brand. Most Internet ideas, most Internet brands, most Internet companies are based on convergence concepts. That's why most Internet brands are likely to fail.

- What if you could find home selection, home buying, home selling, and home mortgages at one-easy-to-use Website? (Homeadvisor.com)

- What if you could use your computer to listen to radio broadcasts? All you need are speakers or headphones and audio software. (Spinner.com, Imagineradio.com, Netradio.com)

- What if you could use your computer to watch television broadcasts? (WinTV, AT1 Technologies)

- What if you could use your mobile phone to surf the Web, send and receive e-mail, and transfer data to a PC? (NeoPoint, Nextel, Sprint PCS)

- What if you could use your computer to listen to music? (MP3.com)

"People used to have to go to three or four different places to get something done" is the premise of many of our clients. "With our new Website, they'll be able to do one-stop shopping." (Whoops. Another client that needs to get the convergence speech.)

We get our hair cut and our clothes dry-cleaned at two different places, but we're quite sure that doesn't spell "opportunity" for some would-be entrepreneur. (We used to get our hair cut and our nails done at one place. Now we go to two different places. That's divergence in action.)

Why do things divide? Divergence is consistent with the laws of nature, convergence is not.

In physics, for instance, the law of entropy says the degree of disorder in a closed system always increases. By contrast, a pattern of convergence would make things more orderly.

In biology, the law of evolution holds that new species are created by divergence of a single species. Convergence, instead, suggests that the combining of two species will yield a new one.

Invariably in nature you see things divide and not converge. We have hundreds of varieties of dogs and hundreds of varieties of cats, but very few catdogs, or chickenducks, or horsecows.

A company goes against the laws of nature when it tries to build an Internet brand on the convergence concept. "Are you getting three different kinds of electronic messages—voice-mail, e-mail, and fax? Fine, we can fix that for you."

These new all-in-one services are called "unified messaging sites." Instead of having to dial into your voice-mail, open your e-mail, or check your fax machine, you just go to the sponsor's Web page and get all your messages (Messagesclick.com, Onebox.com, Telebot.com, mReach.com).

What's wrong with a unified messaging service? Nothing, except it drives like a boat and floats like a car.

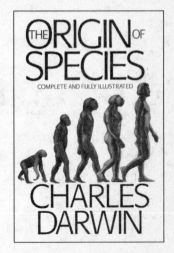

Charles Darwin wrote the book on divergence. New species are created by divergence, writes Darwin, not by convergence of existing species.

11 THE LAW OF TRANSFORMATION

The Internet revolution will transform
all aspects of our lives.

In business there is never only one way to do anything.

- Some people prefer to shop in specialty stores, some people in department stores.

- Some people prefer to shop in supermarkets, some in neighborhood stores.

- Some people love shopping malls, some don't.

- Some people love to buy from catalogs, some don't.

- Some people go to Wal-Mart because the prices are low. Some people go to Neiman-Marcus because the prices are high.

- Some people will turn to the Internet for much of their shopping, information, and communication needs. Some people won't.

- Some products and services will be sold or distributed primarily over the Internet. Some products and services won't.

If your product or service is in the latter category, you might think that you have nothing to gain from the Net. But, in our opinion, you would be wrong.

The Internet will affect your business whether you jump on the Web or not. What changes will the Internet bring to your business and your life? The future is always fuzzy, but here are some predictions.

1. PAPER DIRECTORIES ARE DOOMED.

You won't be surprised to learn that the *Encyclopaedia Britannica*, published since 1768, will no longer be available in a paper version. From now on the encyclopedia will only be available online or on CD-ROM.

The companies that publish "yellow pages" telephone directories ought to be concerned. The fingers that used to go walking though those directories are now moving to the keyboard.

"Information at your fingertips," said Microsoft in its early advertising efforts. And it's true. The plumber, the electrician, the veterinarian, and the auto dealer can be more quickly found and evaluated on an electronic directory than on a paper one.

What will happen to the $12 billion that companies spend annually on yellow-pages advertising? Good question. We'd be concerned if we made our living publishing or selling space in a paper directory.

Paper directories are doomed because of the interactivity of the Internet. The user can manipulate a single computer database in literally thousands of ways.

Furthermore, the database can be updated daily, even hourly. A typical "yellow pages" directory comes out once a year and is out-of-date the day it lands on your doorstep.

Even some great paper institutions are going to have trouble competing in the future. The 116-year-old full *Oxford English Dictionary* could cease to exist after it goes online on a subscription basis. The dictionary, which runs to twenty volumes and costs $2,900, is a dinosaur in the Internet age.

One likely long-term victim of the Internet revolution is the "yellow page" telephone directory. Not only will electronic yellow pages be more convenient to use, they will also be able to offer additional services, such as restaurant reservations, driving directions, and product comparisons.

Electronic catalogs have a number of advantages over paper catalogs like this J.Crew one. They're less expensive to produce and often easier to use. Furthermore, their interactivity allows the user to focus quickly on the products he or she is most interested in buying.

By opening a Website and a chain of retail stores, cataloger L.L. Bean is slowly becoming an unfocused brand. A better strategy for the company might be to become an Internet-only retailer.

2. PAPER CATALOGS FACE AN UNCERTAIN FUTURE.

Mailboxes across the county are stuffed with countless catalogs every day. According to one estimate, 17.6 billion catalogs were mailed in the U.S. last year. That's sixty-four catalogs for every man, woman, and child.

That may change. Catalogs of all types will find themselves under severe electronic competition. There are a number of reasons why a Web catalog is superior to a paper one.

An electronic catalog can be interactive. You can sort by types, by sizes, by colors, by prices, by weights, and so on. Think Amazon.com, for example. You can sort by author, by title, by subject, by category. In contrast, a paper catalog of books is so impractical that few are printed and distributed, except for narrow selections.

Furthermore, an electronic catalog is much less expensive to distribute. Once the material is composed in an electronic format, the cost of distribution is essentially zero. Manufacturing a paper catalog, however, can be costly. Just to print those 17.6 billion mail-order missiles requires 3.35 million tons of paper.

So what do you do if you're L.L. Bean? Good question.

Sales have been essentially flat at L.L. Bean for the last few years. That puts pressure on the bottom line because the company prints and mails catalogs thirty times a year. And printing and mailing costs continue to rise.

So L.L. Bean opens up a Website to sell the same merchandise found in the catalog. Is this a good idea or not?

Yes and no. In general, when you broaden the scope of a brand, you weaken the brand. In the long run, multiple distribution channels substantially increase costs and do not do much to increase sales.

A fully functioning Website with computer hardware and service people backed by a programming staff is not an inexpensive proposition.

To get the company moving again, L.L. Bean is opening

a chain of retail stores, in addition to its nine factory outlet stores. Outlets are one thing, they help you get rid of left-overs. When you open retail stores, however, you are competing directly with yourself, never a good idea.

A better solution for L.L. Bean and other catalog companies is to shift the entire operation to the Web. Don't try to maintain two expensive distribution channels for a brand whose market is limited.

You can't do this overnight. You need transition time. We would gradually reduce the number of catalogs mailed and shift some of the savings into publicity and advertising programs for the Website. You need a way to drive prospects to your site.

One of the major advantages of ordering products from a computer rather than from a catalog is the interactivity of the Website. You know instantly whether or not the product is in stock in the color and size you want.

This, of course, is only a theoretical advantage. Many sites have yet to integrate their warehousing operations with their order-entry systems. When you call to order from a catalog, inevitably at least one of the items you want is out of stock or back-ordered.

Should every catalog company shift to the Web? Of course not. There is never only one way to do anything. For certain products in certain categories, the better strategy might be to remain a catalog-only company. As catalog mailings taper off, the remaining companies in the field will find that their individual catalogs have become more productive.

3. THE ELABORATE FULL-COLOR BROCHURE WILL BECOME EXCEEDINGLY RARE.

Many companies will rethink their use of expensive brochures, which are virtually out-of-date the day they come off the press. It's a lot more efficient to let a prospect

Will the expensive corporate annual report (like this Alcoa 2000 report) become a relic of the past? It looks like it might.

stroll through your Website to look at the same information.

If something catches the prospect's eye, they can always print out the page using one of the many inexpensive color printers now on the market.

One way to promote a seminar, for example, is to send out inexpensive mass mailings (postcards maybe) and then invite prospects to get all the details on your Website.

Annual reports of corporations are another category of printed brochure that is headed for extinction. It may take a while, however, for the Securities and Exchange Commission to change the regulations that govern their use.

4. CLASSIFIED ADVERTISING WILL SHIFT TO THE WEB.

A big chunk of newspapers' revenues comes from their classified advertising. This is a category that will come under immense pressure from the Web. Houses, apartments, and job listings, in particular.

Take the help-wanted category, for example. The first Website to tackle this category was Monster.com, which today leads the Web in online job listings.

Monster.com boasts 800,000 job ads and a database of 16 million resumes. What's more, Monster.com is profitable, having racked up twelve consecutive profitable quarters. In a recent quarter, the site generated $33 million in operating profit on $129 million in revenue.

Long term, the Internet will seriously erode classified advertising, a major source of local newspaper revenues. What should the *Daily Bugle* do about this?

In retrospect the answer is easy. Open a job-listing Website before Monster.com came on the scene. Who knows more about the help-wanted market than the newspaper industry? The companies that spend money today with Monster.com have been their customers for years.

That's the way it often is. The people who know the most about a given market or industry are often the least likely to

---

Newspaper revenues.
Retail ads........ $18 billion
National ads........ 7 billion
Classified ads.....17 billion

Classified advertising is a $17 billion annual business for America's newspapers, or 40 percent of their total advertising revenues. This huge piece of business is highly vulnerable to Internet competition.

see change coming. The motto of many major corporations is: "Hear no change. See no change. Speak no change."

5. THE POSTAL SERVICE WON'T BE DELIVERING AS MUCH MAIL.

The words "Letter Carrier" used to be prominently displayed on postal service uniforms. No more. Today the average letter carrier doesn't carry very many letters. That business has gone electronic, either to phone, facsimile, or e-mail.

In a recent year, more than four trillion e-mail messages were sent, more than forty times the 99.7 billion pieces of first-class mail delivered by the postal service.

The largest segment of first-class mail today is bills, invoices, and financial statements. The sending and paying of bills alone accounts for $17 billion, or almost 30 percent of the postal service's revenue. That segment is going to be especially vulnerable to the Internet.

Look at what happens when a company bills a customer for a product or service the customer has ordered—for example, a telephone company's monthly phone bill.

The telephone company's mainframe computer prints out an invoice, which is stuffed into an envelope, and first-class postage is applied. After the postal service delivers the bill, the customer writes a check, puts it in the return envelope, and adds a first-class postage stamp. After the postal service delivers the envelope, the phone company opens the envelope and deposits the check in its bank account. (So far the roundtrip postage alone has cost sixty-eight cents, minus the postal service's small discount for presorted first-class mail.)

What happens next is the interesting part. The bank's computers make an upward adjustment in the amount of money in the phone company's account and a downward adjustment in the amount of money in the customer's account. (This, of course, is the case when both the seller

If you can't lick 'em, join 'em. The U.S. Postal Service is setting up a Website (eBillPay.com) to try to compete with the bill-paying services that threaten their lucrative first-class-mail business.

and buyer use the same bank. Otherwise some transactions between banks are necessary.)

All that paperwork, all that postage, all that human effort just to shift a number in a computer from Column A to Column B.

People forget that money, for the most part, is not steel engravings printed on paper. It's not even gold in a vault. Money is electronic bits of information stored on computers around the world. To shift money from one account to another, you shift the bits.

The sending and paying of bills online is an idea whose time has come. We foresee a constant rise in electronic banking and a constant decline in the number of pieces of first-class mail sent and received. This is a trend that can't be stopped.

If you think that can't happen soon, look at the phenomenal rise in e-mail, which is increasing at the rate of almost 50 percent a year. Can e-banking be far behind?

According to a recent report issued by the General Accounting Office, "The Postal Service may be nearing the end of an era."

6. FINANCIAL SERVICES OF ALL TYPES WILL SHIFT TO THE WEB.

Because money is nothing more than bits on a computer, the entire financial services industry is headed for the Internet.

It just makes sense to have your bank account in your bedroom or office, where you can check invoices, pay bills, shift funds, and borrow money, all by manipulating bits on a bank's computer.

The computer revolutionized the banking industry once before with the introduction of the automated teller machine. What the ATM has started, the computer (in combination with the Internet) will finish. There's no reason why banking and most financial transactions, including insurance and stock brokerage, should not be handled on the Internet.

Shifting financial transactions to the Internet can result in substantial savings. It costs, on average, one-tenth as much for a bank to handle a financial transaction on the Web as it does on an ATM machine. And one-fortieth as much on the Web as with a teller in the bank itself.

That's the tip of the financial iceberg. The real savings will come from invoicing and bill paying. About seventy billion checks are issued in the United States every year. (That's 260 checks for every person.) Much of this paper blizzard can be easily moved to the Net, saving money and improving the record keeping of both businesses and individuals.

One concern, of course, is the inability of your computer to deal out real money the way an ATM machine does. But this might not turn out to be much of a problem. Paper money is declining in importance as more people shift to credit, debit, and check cards for the bulk of their purchases.

You can spend a week on the road (and we have) without using paper money, with the exception of small bills for tips, taxis, and newspapers. And even taxicab companies are starting to take credit cards.

It will probably be some time before bell-men at hotels or porters at airports swipe credit cards. (With credit cards, they would have to declare all of their tip income on their tax returns.)

7. THE PARCEL DELIVERY BUSINESS WILL SOAR.

The Internet will greatly stimulate business for all of the parcel delivery companies. UPS (United Parcel Service) might want to consider changing its name to IPS (Internet Parcel Service).

As a result of the increases in parcel volume, you can expect delivery prices to hold steady or even decline.

The world leader in cross-border express deliveries is DHL Worldwide Express, which serves nearly 230 countries and territories with a fleet of more than 220 aircraft. DHL also operates a logistics management service that includes Internet tracking and order fulfillment.

The weak link in the system is the front door of the customer. With so many DINK (double income, no kids) families in the country, many customers will not be home when the delivery person arrives.

Some companies are already working on this problem. Smartbox, for example, is a locked, reinforced box that comes in various sizes and sits outside your home. To allow access to all delivery services, the device will be wired to the Internet. When the box owner makes an online purchase, special software will create and transmit a code for each order. A delivery driver can punch in the code on a keypad to unlock the box and make the delivery.

8. INTERNET RETAILING WILL BECOME A PRICE GAME.

Will most products be bought in cyberspace? Probably not. But the Internet will drastically change the focus of most retailers.

Some retailers are worried. Home Depot, which is on the verge of selling its own products over the Internet, is rapping the knuckles of suppliers that have similar dreams. The retailer recently sent a letter to all of its vendors telling them to think twice before selling their tools and equipment directly to consumers through their Websites.

"We think it is shortsighted for vendors to ignore the added value that our retail stores contribute to the sales of their products," stated the Home Depot letter.

The company is worried that their vendors will sell products on the Web at prices lower than Home Depot. And they should be worried. The Internet is inherently a less expensive way to distribute a product or service.

The retail price game causes many problems for manufacturers. Retailers often demand exclusivity in their territories so they can advertise "the lowest price in town." Manufacturers go along with these demands by producing a bewildering variety of models, colors, and sizes. (Mattress and bedding makers are notorious in this respect.)

Wal-Mart and the mass merchandisers are known for demanding special sizes so they can get bigger discounts and customers can't as easily compare prices with the same products at other retail stores. Then there are special purchases, end-of-product runs, obsolete products, manufacturers' seconds, and a host of other strategies for generating low prices on the retail floor. There are also gray-market products brought in from other countries. (Which is why you might see a Mach 3 razor in Costco with the package printed in French.)

The Internet will change the nature of retailing by pulling the plug on many of these "price" promotions. If all the customer really wants is the absolute lowest price, then the place to shop is the Net.

Instead of reading a lot of different ads or driving from store to store, a prospect can sit down at a keyboard and quickly compare prices on a similar item from a large number of sources.

Furthermore, you can also use an "agent" to help you. Agent companies like ClickTheButton, DealPilot, and RUSure have developed software that will scan various shopping sites for price and delivery data, then sort the information (most often by price).

DealTime.com, for example, advertises that it helps you find "exactly what you want, at the price you want, wherever you want." BookPricer.com will help you find "the lowest price for any book in under 30 seconds."

Speaking of books, Amazon.com was discounting bestsellers by up to 40 percent. Booksamillion.com knocks 46 percent off bestsellers. (Some publishers don't give their own authors that big a discount. We should know.)

Then there's Buy.com with the tag line "The lowest prices on Earth." The company is ruthlessly committed to

55% off.
now do you believe in magic?

Members used to get 55 percent off the top ten bestsellers at Booksamillion.com. (It's now down to 46 percent.) Is this strategy effective? To a limited extent, it is. But low prices alone are not enough. You have to have the perception in the mind that your site features low prices, which is what Amazon.com has. If Amazon should ever lose this perception, then there would be an empty void that Booksamillion could fill.

being the price leader, even if this means losing money on every sale. Its technology searches competitors' sites to make sure Buy.com has the lowest prices on the Web. Recently the Palm III Organizer sold for $249 on Buy.com, $330 at CompUSA, and $369 at the manufacturer's own Website.

Buy.com was the fastest-growing company in U.S. history. Unfortunately, it hasn't figured out how to make money. In a recent year the company did $788 million in sales, yet managed to lose $133 million. Will Buy.com become Bankrupt.com?

And look at the personal computer market. With Dell and Gateway doing a big business on the Web, physical retailers selling PCs have been under pressure.

CompUSA, the only physical retailer devoted mainly to personal computers, closed 14 of its 211 superstores. The Good Guys, which operates eighty consumer electronics stores in the West, announced that it was leaving the PC business altogether.

Bear with us. Physical retailing has nothing to fear from the Internet. But it has to change its current emphasis on low price. It has to find a new focus.

9. OUTERNET RETAILING WILL BECOME A SERVICE GAME.

Just as the rise of national brands put pressure on Sears to change its strategy, the rise of the Internet will put pressure on retailers to change their strategies, too.

What retail strategies will work in the shadow of the Internet? We believe the successful retailer of the future will need to play a service game, not a price game. What you might call the Nordstrom approach. (There's no way a physical retailer can compete with an Internet retailer on price.)

The successful outernet retailer of the future will have to emphasize the twin aspects of the physical experience:

This is the Nordstrom employee handbook, a five-by-seven-inch card with the "rules" printed on the back side. "Rule No. 1: Use your good judgment in all situations. There will be no additional rules." No wonder the service at Nordstrom is so good.

Touch and Time, or what we have been calling "T 'n' T."

The Touch aspect of the T 'n' T strategy involves the ability of the prospect to hold, feel, taste, smell, handle, and try the product, not just see and read about it. (After all, you can see the product in full color on the Internet.)

Many retailers will have to make their stores a lot more "touch" friendly. Too many products are locked in glass cabinets or entombed in packaging that greatly discourages handling.

In this connection, Saturn's success in creating a more customer-friendly environment is a good pattern for many traditional retailers to adopt.

The Sharper Image also places a high value on the touch aspect of its stores. Customers are encouraged to touch and try the variety of electronic devices in the store.

The Sephora cosmetic chain is another example of the future of retailing. With its attractive environment, helpful staff, and complete lines, Sephora provides everything a cosmetic buyer might want—except low prices. If you want the absolute lowest cosmetic price, you'll have to go to the Net.

Motion-picture exhibitors have gone through this same process as they have upgraded their facilities to compete with HBO, Showtime, and free movies on television. Now you will find smaller theaters, larger, more comfortable seats, multiplex screens. Even the popcorn is getting better.

Price isn't everything. You can drink beer cheaper at home, but every night the bars in our neighborhood are filled with twentysomethings spending their bundles on Bud Light.

The Time aspect of the T 'n' T strategy seems obvious. Unlike on the Net, you save time when you buy from a physical retailer because you don't have to wait for FedEx or UPS to deliver your purchase.

Yet, the time half of an effective T 'n' T strategy is more subtle than that. In theory you don't wait for your purchases when you buy at retail. But in practice the prospect is often

Like Nordstrom, the Sephora cosmetic chain is another real-world retailer focused on attractive displays and good service. Low prices are not part of the Sephora strategy.

frustrated because the store is out of stock. "Come back next week when our new shipment will be in."

The customer of the future will not tolerate a physical retailer with frequent out-of-stock problems. Many of these problems, of course, stem from the retailer's emphasis on low price, which leads to special deals and special purchases. Abandoning a low-price strategy means that a retailer can concentrate on keeping its inventory up-to-date and complete.

Not counting supermarkets, convenience stores, and similar establishments, roughly half the prospects walk out of a general retail store without buying anything. The major reason is that the store didn't have in stock what the customer wanted.

Most business will probably not be conducted over the Web. But the Internet revolution will force every business to adjust its strategy. From a price game to a service game. T 'n' T, if you will.

10.　INTERNET SEARCH ENGINES WILL DECLINE IN IMPORTANCE.

Search engines like Yahoo! are busy adding functions when they should be battening down the hatches for the rough water ahead. Search engines (or portals) are going to be less important in the future than they were in the past.

Think of it this way. People get to know the Internet brands they want to do business with. When they do, they will go straight to the site instead of making a detour through a search engine. If we want to buy a book, we go to Amazon.com. We don't go to Yahoo! to find out who on the Net sells books.

This view of the future is consistent with one's own personal experience in the real world. Let's say you move to a new community. You might pick up the yellow pages (paper search engine) every time you go out shopping. After you become familiar with the stores in your new community, you make most of your trips without first consulting the yellow pages.

Yahoo! is the welcome wagon on the Internet. Great for the new arrival, but less important for the experienced Internet user.

11. THE INTERNET WILL CHANGE MANY ASPECTS OF THE TELEPHONE INDUSTRY.

In many ways, the Internet and the telephone are similar. Both are information and communications media, but the percentages are different.

If the Internet is 80 percent information and 20 percent communications, the telephone is the opposite. Twenty percent information and 80 percent communications.

The information segment of the telephone medium is a large business in itself even though it accounts for only 20 percent or so of all phone calls. The visible symbol of this information segment, of course, is the yellow pages. "Let your fingers do the walking."

That will change. The Internet will become a direct competitor to the telephone. (Fortunately for the phone companies, most people will continue to use phone lines to connect to the Internet.)

On the communications side, e-mail will replace many phone and fax calls. On the information side, the Net will become an electronic yellow pages.

What television did to radio, the Internet will do to the telephone. TV virtually wiped out entertainment on radio. The Internet will do the same for information on the telephone. Forget 777-FILM and the ten minutes it takes to get playing times for your favorite movie.

For many people the change couldn't come too soon. How many hours have you spent punching in numbers trying to reach someone in Corporate America to help you?

For years the telephone industry has been saying, "Let your fingers do the walking." With the Internet, your fingers can do all the walking, not just some of the walking.

The automated call-routing systems used by most national companies are a disgrace.

First they answer your call with a variety of options. After punching in an endless series of numbers, you get the following message: "All of our representatives are currently helping other customers; the next available agent will be with you shortly."

By removing the human interface, the Internet promises to greatly speed up the information functions formerly handled on the phone.

Airline reservations, movie tickets, reservations for rock concerts and sporting events, and restaurant hours and reservations are just some of the information-related transactions that will be moving from the phone to the Net.

12. THERE WILL BE SPEED BUMPS ON THE INTERNET.

In spite of our rosy predictions, the Internet faces two speed bumps in the near future.

One is the Internet bubble itself. Just because two guys under thirty start a Website with $30 million in venture-capital funds doesn't automatically make the site worth $3 billion. The bubble has burst.

In spite of its enormous acceptance, it's going to be difficult to make money on the Net. The Internet is a high-volume, low-margin medium. In other words, a price game. Investors didn't truly understand the nature of this medium. While the Internet is wildly popular, it will not be wildly profitable. And profit is what Wall Street ultimately seeks.

The Internet will survive and prosper. But many Internet companies will not.

The second speed bump along the way is the tax issue. Currently there is a moratorium on state and federal taxes.

That will change. The 46 states, 4,831 cities, and 1,151 counties that impose sales taxes are not going to give the

Yes, the Internet Bubble did burst, as predicted by a book written by Anthony B. Perkins and Michael C. Perkins. But does this mean the end of the Internet? Not really. The Internet, in our opinion, has a bright future, but that does not necessarily include those people who bought overpriced Internet stocks.

Internet a free ride forever. Sooner or later they are going to want their cut.

The computer we recently purchased on the Net would have cost $111.72 more (to cover taxes) if bought locally. Sooner or later, the governor, the mayor, or the county tax commissioner is going to want to get his or her hands on that $111.72. You can count on it.

What's next? What will come after the Internet? What will be the technological revolution of the first decade of the next millennium? Who knows?

- It could be the optical computer with photons carrying the ball in place of electrons. Such a development could drastically reduce the size and increase the speed and memory capacities of all computing devices, making a mockery of Moore's law.

- It could be a new engine, light in weight, highly efficient, and ultrapowerful. Such a development could revolutionize the transportation industries: automotive, aircraft, shipping, railroad.

- It could be a new development in genetics, especially in the field of agriculture. Such a development could revolutionize the way crops are planted, grown, and harvested.

Whatever the future brings, you can be sure of one thing: It will be a destabilizing development. It will change the way you manage your business and the way you build your brands.

And there will be more immutable laws of branding.

Yahoo!, xiv, 113
   and law of advertising, 179
   and law of globalism,
      187–88
   and law of the generic,
      136
   and law of the proper
      name, 150–51, 162–63
   and law of time, 192–96

and law of transformation,
   232–33
and law of vanity, 202–4,
   206, 208–9
Yang, Jerry, 113, 163
yellow pages, 221,
   232–33

Zippo Corporation, 68–69